I See A New Apostolic Generation

By: Jeremiah Johnson

Cover design by Darin Shiflett
www.lifedesignsandmedia.com

ISBN-13: 978-1979628259

ISBN-10: 1979628254

To order bulk copies of this book or other products from
Jeremiah Johnson, please visit our website at
jeremiahjohnson.tv

Dedication

To my Uncle Christopher Johnson…

Words cannot express my deepest gratitude for the countless hours and years of investments that you have made in my life. Thank you for giving me my love for the Word of God and desire to understand apostolic ministry in greater capacities. You are a true apostolic father to this generation and I'm humbled to have the opportunity to run alongside of you in these marvelous days that we live in. If anyone has benefited from my life and ministry, they most certainly have benefited from yours. I love you!

Please visit: www.fishnet-ministries.com to learn about the life and ministry of Christopher Johnson.

Table of Contents

1. A Trip to Heaven   Page 7
2. Apostolic Order   Page 17
3. The Three Judgments   Page 50
4. The New Wineskin is Forming   Page 82
5. The New Apostolic Generation   Page 104
6. Apostolic Fathering   Page 123
7. Apostolic Christianity   Page 146

Acknowledgments

I would like to thank my precious wife Morgan Johnson for her incredible sacrifices that she has made on this journey that God has called our family on. Thank you for your constant encouragement and flexibility. I love you so much!

Thank you to Barry Nichols and David Vespa, my fellow Elders at Heart of the Father Ministry. Each one of you have radically impacted my life and I'm grateful for your commitment to eldership and doing life together. May our challenges and victories be a great blessing to all those who read this book. I love you and your families very much.

A special thank you to the community of believers at Heart of the Father Ministry in Lakeland, FL. You all have lived through much of this book. Thank you for your grace, your love, and support as I have navigated the call on my life. You have been more of a blessing to me and my family than you will ever know.

Lastly, thank you Father! Thank you Jesus! Thank you most precious Holy Spirit! Where would I be without you?

-1-
A Trip to Heaven

The night was July 14, 2010. That year, I had just planted a church called, "Heart of the Father Ministry" in Lakeland, Florida. At the time, I was very confident in the future of the church and the vision that I was carrying. I had attended a four-year bible college and received a bachelor's degree, grew up around the things of God, and now I was ready to build a church around the gifts and charisma that God had given me. I had every intention of planting a one-man ministry!

As I laid down to sleep that night, I quickly realized that I was not only mistaken concerning what I thought God was calling me to do, and most of what I learned in bible college, but I was in store for the greatest wake up call of my life: an encounter with God that has marked me forever!

The Prophetic Dream

In the dream, I found myself in the most profound prophetic experience I have ever had. I was standing in front of a door that was as tall as my eyes could see. To the left and right of the door was brick stone. I immediately noticed that there was an inscription in the brick to the right of the door that read, "Good shepherds do not treat people like sheep. Shepherds are sheep also, and they need to lead people in the same manner as they themselves are led by the Lord." After I read the inscription aloud in amazement, the large door in front of me opened and I walked into the most beautiful, lively, colorful, and vast place I have ever been to or seen in my life.

Extravagant in regards to what I beheld does not even do it justice! Inside this place was celestial and angelic beings. Some were the size of an average human being and others were extremely large. Many of them had beautifully colored wings and some glowing so bright that I couldn't help but gaze upon the beauty of their splendor. I saw colors and heard sounds that I had previously never encountered or seen to this day. As I began to make my way forward, I realized that I was in no ordinary place. I said out loud in the dream, "This is none other than the heavenly courts!"

As those words left my lips, suddenly, three golden thrones appeared in the distance before me. There was one throne for the Holy Spirit, one for Jesus, and one for the Father. Holy fear began to grip my heart as I locked eyes with the Lord Jesus Christ for the very first time in my life, who was sitting at the right hand of the Father. I began to tremble at the beauty and majesty that was seated before me.

I began to fix my eyes upon the golden throne in the center where the Father was, yet I could not make out His figure. I only knew by the glory and presence that I felt that He was there. I made several steps to try to close the distance between where I was and where the golden thrones were and instantly, seven angels stood at my left and my right. I stood there stunned, gazing into their faces that radiated joy and delight. They smiled at me and looked toward the Father's throne, as did I.

A holy hush fell within the heavenly courts and I heard God the Father's voice. He began to speak to me saying, "The seven angels that stand before Me with you are the seven churches. The seven churches represent my corporate body." He paused and then said, "I summon you; son of man, apostles, prophets, shepherds, teachers, and evangelists: LET MY PEOPLE GO!" As He said, "Let my people go", the courts of heaven shook and His voice thundered. My entire body stiffened and I immediately sensed in the dream that this mandate must precede the second coming of the Lord Jesus. Then I immediately awoke.

Divine Conversation

I sat up in my bed that morning, out of breath and profusely sweating. Deeply afraid and sensing the weight of what I had just experienced, I cried out to the Lord and said, "Father, No! There is no way that you are calling me to apostles, prophets, teachers, shepherds, and evangelists in the earth with a message to, "Let Your People Go!" There was no response, only deafening silence and my mind spinning wildly.

I began to tremble even thinking of telling people that I actually went to heaven. "They are going to label me a false prophet!", I spoke aloud in the silence of my room. I then said to God, "Father, what are your people not doing that you want them to do?" His voice spoke clearly to me and said, "Jeremiah, why did I free My people from Egypt?" I said, "Because you had called them to the Promise Land". He said, "Wrong Answer. Go back and study the book of Exodus and I will meet you there."

I quickly jumped out of my bed and opened up my Bible. I read the entire book of Exodus in one setting that morning and there the answer was before my eyes, time and time again.

Exodus 7:16 ..."Let My people go, that they may **serve Me** in the wilderness"

Exodus 8:1 ..."Let My people go, that they may **serve Me.**"

Exodus 9:1…"Let My people go, that they may **serve Me**."

Exodus 9:13…"Let My people go, that they may **serve Me**."

Exodus 10:3 …"Let My people go, that they may **serve Me**."

After finishing reading the book of Exodus, I found myself arguing with the Lord that day and for many weeks after that. "What are you talking about God? Your people are serving you," I said. Then His words would pierce my heart like an arrow for months on end, "Jeremiah, My people are not serving me, nor are they worshipping me in a way that is pleasing to me, for they have become more comfortable serving men, serving their ministries, and worshipping at their feet than they are serving, ministering, and worshipping Me."

As He would further share His heart concerning these matters, I would experience seasons of great weeping and travail. As I cried out for greater wisdom and revelation concerning this dream, He said to me one day, "Jeremiah, the current wineskin of church leadership in the earth cannot contain the new wine that I am about to pour out in My church. You must tell church leadership to let My people go. They must not accept the worship of the people any longer. I am about to shake the very foundation of the Church. In the years to come, you will see a new apostolic generation rise who will build according to the pattern that I have set forth in Scripture. They will expose the kingdoms of Saul who are building their own names and ministries, and call forth five fold ministry leaders with a Davidic anointing who will walk humbly before Me. If my apostles, prophets, shepherds, teachers, and evangelists will listen to My voice and let the people go, I will reward them with levels of glory that have never been seen before upon the earth. If they refuse, three judgments will fall upon them: family crisis, personal burnout, and moral failure."

I must admit that since the night of that prophetic dream and conversation the following months with the Lord, my life has never been the same. I was about to make one of the biggest mistakes of my life by building a one-man ministry centered around my gifts and calling, but the grace of God spared me! I'm so grateful, but still to this day I have been shaken to my core, and the truth is, I am still feeling the weight of what I was shown even up to this very hour. I have only ever shared that prophetic dream and experience you just read on two public occasions. It has been too much of a fearful and weighty encounter just to share flippantly. I have known in my heart these last seven years that the Holy Spirit must do

His work in me before I release His words through me. I believe now is the time to share this revelation and release a clear sound to the body of Christ so that a new apostolic generation might emerge in the earth who will carry this mandate from God to restore and recover apostolic order to the Church. What kind of apostolic order does God want to bring to the global Church? Keep reading to find out!

-2-
Apostolic Order

"Jeremiah, the new wine that I am about to pour out upon my Bride cannot be contained in the existing one-man ministry structure that the Church has been built upon" said the Lord. This was the revelation the Father gave me concerning His mandate to church leadership to, "Let My People Go." He continued on, "For years, contemporary church leadership has tried to model everything in the book of Acts and the Epistles except the governmental structure that I set in place. Too many are chasing the miracles, the community, and the outpouring of the Holy Spirit, but they will never taste of the new wine I am desiring to send to My Bride unless they learn how to build My house according to My heart and pattern as found in the Scriptures."

Difficult Questions

As I began to seek God and examine the Scriptures to find the "pattern" He kept telling me the new apostolic generation would restore and recover, I was stunned at my findings. I was searching for any place in the New Testament where one set man had control over a church and couldn't find any. I was looking for a senior pastor running a church off of his gifting and charisma and found no passages of Scripture to support this wineskin. After a period of months, I finally came to the startling realization that there is no trace of evidence in support of building one-man ministries anywhere in the New Testament. I was in shock and began asking difficult questions. What if the greatest hindrance to a worldwide revival is not the sin of the world or even the church? What if the greatest obstacle to a genuine move of God is the way our current church leadership models are structured?

This perhaps is the new apostolic generation's greatest assignment and cross to bear in this hour, to entirely re-think and re-examine the Scriptures to discover how to build the house of God in a different way than what we currently see around us. The new apostolic generation emerging will restore and recover what has been lost throughout the centuries concerning church leadership. If they can successfully do this, we will see denominations fall, one-man ministries be stripped of their ego, pride, and arrogance, and the control and manipulation that has enslaved church culture for years finally and ultimately be broken. The Father is saying to church leaders in the earth right now, "Let My People Go" and in order to let His people go, we are going to have to stop building His house around one-man ministries and start building according to the pattern found in the New Testament.

The Biblical Pattern

As previously stated and discovered, nowhere in the New Testament was one man ever set over a body of believers and called their senior pastor. However, what we do find is a plurality of Elders giving leadership to a body of believers by an apostle who planted the church. In every church that was founded in the New Testament, there were multiple men who gave shared oversight of the flock. There was never one man or woman that called the shots, had unilateral authority, and answered to no one. Once the church was planted by an apostle and proper foundation was laid, the oversight and daily affairs were handed over to a plurality of elders who governed the church together as a team. Let's re-examine several passages of Scripture to support such shocking claims:

- Elder(s) governed the church in Jerusalem (Acts 15)

- Elder(s) are found in the churches of Judea and the surrounding area (Acts 11:30; James 5:14,15).

- Plurality of elder(s) were established in the churches of Derbe, Lystra, Iconium, and Antioch (Acts 14:23); in the church at Ephesus (Acts 20:17; 1 Tim 3:1-7; 5:17-25); in the church at Philippi (Phil 1:1); and in the churches on the island of Crete (Titus 1:5)

- According to 1 Peter, a plurality of elder(s) existed in churches throughout northwestern Asia minor: Pontus, Galatia, Cappadocia, Asia, and Bithynia (1 Peter 1:1; 5:1).

Did you know that the New Testament offers more instruction regarding elders in the church than baptism, spiritual gifts, and the Lord's supper? Again, there are so many in the earth right now searching for why we are falling so short of what we read in the book of Acts and the Epistles and I'm sounding the alarm: the way we have chosen to build the house of God as church leaders is our number one limitation and hindrance to a training and equipping of the saints that will usher in the greatest revival and subsequent reformation we have ever known. The global body of Christ is not being trained, equipped, and reaching the fullness of the knowledge of the Son of God because they are only being exposed to the ministry of one man on a consistent basis.

Let's take a look at instructions that were given to the elders and not a senior pastor in the New Testament:

- James instructs those who are sick to call upon the **elders** of the church (James 5:14).
- Paul instructs the Ephesian church to financially support **elders** who labor at "preaching and teaching" (1 Tim 5:17,18).
- Paul instructs the church as to proper qualifications for **eldership** (1 Tim 3:1-7; Titus 1:5-9)

- Peter instructs the young men to submit to the church **elders** (1 Peter 5:5)

- The writer of Hebrews instructs his readers to obey and submit to the **elders** (Heb 13:17)

- Paul instructs the church to acknowledge, love, and live at peace with its **elders** (1 Thess. 5:12,13)

Wayne Grudem in his book *Systematic Theology* says, "No passage in the New Testament suggests that any church, no matter how small, had only one senior leader. The consistent New Testament pattern is a plurality of elders "in every church" (Acts 14:23) and "in every town" (Titus 1:5). We do not see a diversity of forms of government in the New Testament church, but a unified and consistent pattern in which every church had elders governing it and keeping watch over it (Acts 20:28; Heb. 13:17; 1 Peter 5:2-3)." (Systematic Theology, Zondervan Publishing House 1994 page 913)

How can there be so many references to multiple elders giving oversight and leadership to the local church in the New Testament, yet this structure of church leadership can hardly be found in America and many parts of the world? How have we strayed so far from what was considered the normal way of appointing leaders to govern the house of God in the New Testament? Once again, could it be true that the greatest resistance to new wine being poured out upon this generation is the one-man ministries we have built? Are we asking God to fill a church model He never formed and created to begin with?

Elders and the Five-Fold Ministry

From what we have just read in the New Testament, the pattern revealed to us is one in which apostles are called to establish a plurality of elders in the house of God because it is the gateway to the five-fold ministry being fully operational. Having multiple elders governing a body of believers, as opposed to one man, protects the headship of Jesus Christ so that only He may receive pre-eminence. Bible scholar Wayne Grudem writes again and says, "A practical problem with a 'single man' system is either an excessive concentration of power in one person or excessive demands laid upon him. In either case, the temptations to sin are very great. It was never the pattern in the New Testament, even with the apostles, to concentrate ruling power in the hands of any one person." (Systematic Theology, Zondervaan Publishing House 1994 page 931)

In order to be on an eldership team, one must have a five-fold ministry call on their life. The term "elder" in the contemporary body of Christ has become wrongly reserved for an older man who has enough money or wisdom in a church to influence people. When Paul wrote to Titus regarding qualifications for elders, one of them was that an elder must, "hold fast to the faithful word which is in accordance with the teaching, that he may be able both to exhort in sound doctrine and to refute those who contradict." (Titus 1:9) Therefore, elders must be able to teach and defend the Word of God, which is evidence of a five-fold ministry call upon their lives. If an elder at a church does not have a "word" ministry, they are not biblically qualified to be one.

It is also important to note that someone must have a five-fold ministry calling to be an elder, but someone can also have a five-fold ministry calling and not be an elder. The work of eldership is to be desired (1 Tim 3:1) and also a responsibility that requires proper shepherding of the flock of God. (1 Peter 5:2) An individual with a five-fold ministry call that does not believe they have the necessary time and sacrifice in order to be an elder, can still function in their calling without being an elder.

As apostles plant churches and establish eldership teams who have a five-fold ministry call on their lives, a training and equipping of the saints is allowed to take place that is simply impossible with a one-man ministry running the show. As exemplified by Paul, the apostle who planted the church typically moves on to plant another one after he has laid Jesus Christ as the foundation, cornerstone, and head of His Church, and established a plurality of elders to govern the affairs of the church. If the apostle who planted the church chooses to remain at the church that he planted among the eldership team, he becomes a fellow elder who functions apostolically in their midst, but he cannot usurp the elders, or be domineering over them. He must choose to come alongside of them so that the five-fold ministry might be fully expressed in the body of believers. (1 Peter 5:1)

Apostolic Order in Lakeland, FL

After being taken to heaven and receiving the life changing dream and encounter with the Lord in 2010, searching the Scriptures for myself in the days that followed, and then seeking the wisdom and counsel of spiritual fathers, we began to form a plurality of elders at Heart of the Father Ministry, the church I planted. Introducing a biblical model of church leadership to the public was extremely difficult in the early years. As the apostle and founder of the church, I had to choose to be a fellow elder with two other men and learn how to govern the flock of God on a completely shared system of leadership with Jesus Christ as our senior pastor.

No one elder has unilateral authority, nor is there voting on any issues. We simply dialogue to unity. We currently have fourteen deacon couples who serve in specific volunteer capacities within our community of a little more than four hundred members. People often ask me how I minister around the nation and the world, and also be involved in a local church. The answer is simple: plurality of eldership. Heart of the Father Ministry in Lakeland, FL does not revolve around my gifting, or any one of the elders, because leadership is shared in every way and built upon the foundation of Jesus Christ.

Over the years, I have traveled and ministered with numerous "senior pastors" of churches who have struggled with the call on their life because of how they have chosen to build the house of God. When they are ministering away from home tithes and offerings are typically down, and so is attendance, because they have built their ministry off their gifting and charisma. I have also met many burned out church leaders who planted churches and desired to travel later in life, but simply could not because they failed to establish a plurality of elders in their congregation that could share the leadership together!

Over the last seven years, our eldership team has learned, and is learning, how to build love relationship with one another outside all "ministry". We each have a unique grace and five-fold ministry call on our lives that determines our function in the community. We serve and lead through relationship with one another and the community, never hierarchy and control. There are no titles in any form, just first names. I have never asked anyone to call me apostle or prophet anything. Just Jeremiah. There is no need to because we simply have a commitment to keep our eyes fixed on Jesus Christ. We recognize one another's five-fold ministry call, but choose to walk as sons to the Father, and brothers and friends with one another, before serving in ministry together.

Divine Tension

As an elder on a team of men who have different five-fold ministry callings, I understand the tension that can exist because of the grace on each one of our lives. If you sat an apostle, prophet, teacher, shepherd, and evangelist down and asked them what God was saying to His Church, each of them would give you a different answer because of the grace of God on their lives. The apostle would say the Church needs more fathering, order, power, and administration. The prophet would say the Church needs to grow in the Spirit, and learn how to prophesy and operate in the gifts. The teacher would say that the Church needs to learn the Word of God more. The shepherd would say that people are hurting and broken, and need counseling and wisdom. The evangelist would say people are dying and going to hell, and we need to feed the poor! What a beautiful thing it is to have different ministries carrying five different portions of who Jesus Christ is, yet called to work together in unity! It is a beautiful thing when apostles, prophets, teachers, shepherds, and evangelists start working together in one community of believers! Plurality of eldership does not minimize one another's gifting, but actually maximizes it!

The vision and direction of each church plant, governed by the plurality of elders, is going to be determined by what five-fold ministry calling the elders have. In other words, each local church expression is going to have a certain flavor because of the shared leadership of the eldership team. We know in the church of Antioch, there were prophets and teachers which would have given them a unique anointing. (Acts 13:1) Rather than a domineering vision from one man, churches that are governed by eldership teams have shared vision and purpose. It's exciting and a tremendous opportunity for so much training and equipping of the saints, but learning how to work through the tension that five-fold ministers feel on some days is both healthy and necessary.

Each one of our elders at Heart of the Father Ministry functions according to the grace God has given us, including a weekly preaching rotation, counseling appointments, discipleship, and caring for the flock. Many visitors are stunned to visit our church and find out that as a national and international conference speaker, I am not speaking at the church that Sunday or Wednesday. I'm actually receiving the Word from one of our elders and spending time with my family. Again, no one elder calls all the shots, or carries the community on his own shoulders. We meet weekly to pray together, fast as needed, and build deep love and relationship with one another. The truth is that jealousy, insecurity, and pride will not survive plurality of eldership. As I have preached and taught across the world and shared on the biblical model for church leadership, senior pastors of churches always raise their hands and ask, "Jeremiah, who is in control in Lakeland? Come on, you are the apostle and you just have a board of elders right?" My response continues to shock them. "No! Plurality of eldership is not about control, it's learning how to function together as a team in the midst of the tension you feel on days because you each have a different five-fold ministry call on your life. It's all about Jesus and developing authentic relationship and accountability like you've never seen before."

I love what Alexander Strauch writes and says concerning plurality of eldership, because we have and are still very much submitting to this process that he so eloquently describes: "Establishing healthy biblical eldership requires the elders to show mutual regard and concern for one another, submit themselves to one another, patiently wait upon one another, and defer and prefer one another. Eldership thus enhances brotherly love, humility, and mutuality. Learning how to lead and care for the flock together will expose impatience with one another, stubbornness, bull-headedness, selfish-immaturity, domineering dispositions, prayerlessness, pride, and jealousy." (Biblical Eldership, Lewis and Roth Publishers 1995 page 45)

Apostolic Grace

Each of the five ministries that God has given to His church in Ephesians 4:11(apostles, prophets, teachers, shepherds, and evangelists) have a specific grace upon their lives that determines their function. For example,

Ephesians 2:20 says that the foundation of the Church is built upon the apostles and prophets. In other words, the two ministries of apostles and prophets carry unique grace to lay foundation in the house of God that teachers, shepherds, and evangelists cannot because of the grace God has given them. While apostles and prophets are foundation layers, teachers, shepherds, and evangelists have building ministries. Where in the New Testament do you ever find a pastor or evangelist planting a church?

One of the primary issues in the contemporary church culture is that we have attempted to establish the house of God with teachers, shepherds, and evangelists (building ministries) without the foundational ministries of apostles and prophets. Reaping what we have sown, we now have a global Church that in many places is a mile wide and an inch deep. It looks beautiful on the outside, but the foundation is crumbling because of the way we have chosen to build. When Jesus Christ returns, will He say to us "Well done!" or "What have you done?"

Foundation Layers

Please do not misunderstand what I am saying. Apostles and prophets are not better than teachers, shepherds, and evangelists. This is not a competition, nor is it a hierarchy. We are discussing the sequence of properly building the wineskin that will hold the new wine God has always desired to pour out in every generation. This is about recognizing the grace that is upon certain ministries and allowing them the function according to the pattern laid out in Scripture. Not every individual that graduates from bible college and seminary is a "pastor". Not every person who enters into ministry is a "teacher". What happens if they are called by God and given grace to be an "apostle" or "prophet"? Our religious denominations do not have room, or even a paradigm, for such biblical foundations!

1 Corinthians 12:28 says, "And God has appointed in the church, first apostles, second prophets, third teachers, then miracles, then gifts of healing, helps, administrations, and various kinds of tongues." Why has God first appointed apostles and then prophets in the Church? Because they alone carry the grace and blueprints to lay proper foundation in the Church. What exactly is that grace?

Paul, a called apostle says in 1 Corinthians 3:10-11, "According to the grace of God which was given to me, as a wise masterbuilder I laid a foundation, and another is building upon it. But let each man be careful how he builds upon it. For no man can lay a foundation other than the one which is laid, which is Jesus Christ."

Apostles Reveal Jesus Christ

Apostolic grace was given to Paul to uncover and unveil the true foundation of the Church, Jesus Christ. Apostles carry specific and unique grace to reveal the person of Jesus to His body. Apostolic preaching is the preaching of Christ and Him crucified. If we cancel and negate the ministry of apostles in the body of Christ, then we are removing the very individuals who carry the grace to connect us to our true head, source, foundation, and cornerstone: Jesus Christ! I recently read an article by a well known "apostle" in the body of Christ who listed fifteen functions of apostles. There was not a single mention of revealing Jesus Christ to His body in the list. How far our modern day apostolic ministry has fallen from the example and blueprint Paul left us in Scripture!

Paul goes on to say, "Now if any man builds upon the foundation with gold, silver, precious stones, wood, hay, straw, each man's work will become evident; for the day will show it, because it is to be revealed with fire: and the fire itself will test the quality of each man's work" (1 Cor 3:12-13).

There is a tangible fire that is going to come and consume the global Church. How we have chosen to build the house of God will be exposed. Where there are no apostles and apostolic grace functioning, Jesus Christ is not being revealed for who He really is. It is also noteworthy that in this same chapter, Paul also addresses the tendency for apostolic ministry to turn into a cult following. We not only need apostolic order to return to the Church so that Jesus might take pre-eminence in all things, but we also need so called "apostles" who are building their own kingdoms and ministries to repent and step aside. The problem with much of our contemporary apostolic ministry is that it brings a 'takeover' mentality to the Church where so called "apostles" build cult like followings after themselves. They operate in a Diotrephes spirit and want first place in all things. (3 John 1:9). This is a tremendous tragedy because apostles are the ones who actually carry the grace to connect the body to our true head, Jesus Christ.

I believe one of the greatest misunderstandings that people have about true apostles is that they fail to recognize that this ministry will not build upon any other foundation than Jesus Christ. (Eph 2:20) True apostles will tear down any other foundation besides Jesus Christ that they encounter in the house of God. If a ministry or church has been built upon someone's gifting, personality, or charisma, a true apostle will call it out and tear it down. If a ministry or church has been built by pastors and teachers and has no revelation of Jesus Christ, a true apostle will expose the faulty foundations and seek to establish apostolic order within the body. Many church leaders want to invite the ministry of apostles in their midst, but if that church is not founded on Jesus there is going to be a tremendous amount of apostolic order that will need to be established.

Apostles Do More Than Plant Churches

A large portion of apostolic grace is the setting of things into proper order and function (1 Cor 11:34). For example, apostles establish the doctrines of Christ, they father, they correct defects, ordain elders, uproot and tear down false doctrines, and challenge false teachers. This mandate requires great time and effort on their part in one community of believers.

Apostles are wise master builders (1 Cor 3:10). In other words, when they detect that a proper foundation has not been laid (Jesus Christ as the cornerstone and foundation), they will overthrow, uproot, tear down, and destroy before they begin to build and bring multiplication. It is for this reason that perhaps true apostles are not invited into many existing church structures because of the evident grace upon their lives.

Rather than having a couple of "revival services" over a weekend, true apostles will inquire and ask the hard questions to eldership teams, not blow in and out over a weekend for a quick honorarium. Apostles carry a tremendous father's heart that is concerned for the welfare of those they are called to minister to. The truth be told, apostolic work is extremely difficult and oftentimes takes years! Paul didn't spend a weekend in Ephesus, he spent three years, and on and on in other cities and regions. Calling people "apostles" who blow in and out of cities and have no hand in actually building and establishing the house of God on a consistent basis is absurd! Even worse, there are so called "apostles" floating around the earth right now claiming apostolic grace who have never planted a church, laid hands on eldership teams, nor fathered the five-fold ministry.

I see God releasing and raising up a new apostolic generation who are sound in the doctrines of Christ, who carry a specific anointing to set a body of believers into proper order and function, and they are radically committed to spending lengthy amounts of time and care for those God has called them to. The foundation and revelation of Jesus Christ must return to the global Church in this hour, and the new apostolic generation has been graced by God to bring forth this awakening and reformation.

The Headship of Jesus Christ

Why is the current, contemporary church leadership structure, where one man or woman runs the show and calls the shots, such a limitation and hindrance to the glory that God wants to send the church? Why is the Father in Heaven saying to Apostles, Prophets, Teachers, Shepherds, and Evangelists, "Let My People Go"?

I believe the answer is found in the fact that Jesus Christ must receive the service and worship that only He, and He alone, deserves. In the first century, no leader would dare take the position or title of sole ruler, overseer, or head of the church. Alexander Strauch puts it like this, "We Christians today, however, are so accustomed to speaking of 'the pastor' that we do not stop and realize that the New Testament does not. This fact is profoundly significant, and we must not permit our customary practice to shield our minds from this important truth. There is only one flock and one Pastor (John 10:16), one body and one

Head (Col. 1:18), one holy priesthood and one great High

Priest (Heb 4:14), one brotherhood and one Elder Brother

(Rom. 8:29), one building and one Cornerstone (1 Peter

2:5), one Mediator, one Lord. Jesus Christ is "Senior

Pastor", and all others are His under shepherds (1 Peter

5:4)" (Biblical Eldership, Lewis and Roth Publishers 1995

page 115).

The reason why Jesus Christ has a huge problem

with the way our contemporary church leadership

structures have been built is because it takes the worship

and service off of Him and places it upon mere men. One-

man ministries are often times guilty of calling disciples

after themselves and stealing the glory that only Jesus

Christ deserves. This is why in every church in the New

Testament multiple elders were set in place to oversee the

people, so that one man would not become the focus and need of/for the people.

As Robert Greenleaf in his book *Servant Leadership* says, "To be a lone chief atop a pyramid is abnormal and corrupting. None of us are perfect by ourselves, and all of us need the help and correcting influence of close colleagues. When someone is moved atop a pyramid, that person no longer has colleagues, only subordinates. Even the frankest and bravest subordinates do not talk with their boss in the same way that they talk with colleagues who are equals, and normal communication patterns become warped" (Biblical Eldership, Lewis and Roth Publishers 1995 page 41).

Biblical eldership guards and promotes the pre-eminence and position of Jesus Christ over the local church. It brings accountability and relationship to five-fold ministry leaders that building one-man ministries simply cannot. The first century church was Christ-centered and Christ-dependent. The centrality of Jesus Christ in all things was the fuel for the glory that they walked in on a daily basis. The new apostolic generation emerging will recover and restore plurality of eldership back to the Church. They will challenge one-man ministries to "Let the People Go" so that a training and equipping of the five-fold ministry can take place like never before. Unfortunately, there will be those who refuse to reform their ways and continue on in the religious traditions of men. They will not build according to the pattern clearly set forth in Scripture. They will vehemently resent and resist the message and mandate of this book and the criticism and attacks will be fierce. After my experience in heaven, season of revelation, and search of the Scriptures that followed, God said to me that there were three judgments that He has released upon those who have chosen to build one-man ministries. Let's look at

them closely now in the next chapter.

-3-
The Three Judgments

As I have sought God with a broken heart and many tears concerning his three primary judgments that He has released upon church leaders who have chosen to build one-man ministries, He has continually reminded me of the leadership of King Saul, and how radically different it was compared to King David. I believe the spirit that King Saul walked in mirrors the spirit that one-man ministries carry. On the other hand, those who will begin to form a new wineskin led by a plurality of elders will carry a Davidic heart and spirit.

One of the great enemies of the new apostolic generation will be church leaders operating in a Saul spirit who are building their own kingdoms in the body of Christ, and desiring to take pre-eminence in all things.

They will resist plurality of eldership, which is the gateway to the restoration of the five-fold ministry in the body, and they will loathe the exaltation of Jesus Christ in all things, as their cult following is exposed for what it really is.

Before we look at the three judgments that fall upon church leaders who choose to build their own one-man ministries, I would like to share an encounter that I had with God concerning the kingdom of Saul versus the kingdom of David.

The Kingdom of Saul

In June 2013, I attended eight revival services where thousands of people, including pastors and leaders, gathered to receive a fresh touch of fire upon their lives and ministries. One night as I was observing hundreds of church leaders responding to an altar call, I suddenly had an open vision and heard the audible voice of the Father. In the vision, I was shown a large mountain where thousands of pastors and leaders were falling on their own swords. It was a horrifying scene to be sure. The next thing that I saw was a young man in a cave, crying out and weeping before the Lord. Then I heard the Father speak this phrase to me that I have never seen or heard before: "I do not hear the cries that come from Mt. Gilboa, but I do hear the cries that come from Engedi."

As these words from the Father began to sink into the depths of my heart, I began to weep and wail. I knew that the Father was showing me where many church leaders are headed- for Mt. Gilboa- where King Saul fell upon his own sword. Yet, I was also filled with hope, realizing that the cries from Engedi, the very place where young David humbled Himself and refused to be promoted unless it be from the hand of the Father, would be heard.

7 Signs that Church Leaders are Headed for Mt. Gilboa

Out of this encounter with the Lord, He revealed to me that there are seven specific signs that mark the life and ministry of a church leader who is headed for Mount Gilboa. They are as follows:

1. Insensitivity of Heart (1 Samuel 13:5-14)

30,000 chariots, 6,000 horsemen, and Philistines that outnumbered the sand on the seashore camped at Michmash against King Saul and the people of Israel. Samuel the prophet had mandated that Israel wait 7 days until his arrival to offer sacrifices to the Lord before the day of battle. After 7 days passed and Samuel did not arrive as scheduled, King Saul took matters into his own hands, forcing himself to offer the sacrifices, which was a violation of the law. Upon Samuel's late arrival he said to Saul, "You have acted foolishly, you have not kept the commandments of the Lord your God, which He commanded you, for now the Lord would have established your kingdom over Israel forever. But now your kingdom shall not endure. The Lord has sought out for Himself a man after His own heart, and the Lord has appointed him as ruler over His people, because you have not kept what the Lord commanded you."

Church leaders headed for Mt. Gilboa mistake the silence, and often time vagueness of God, as a sign to take matters into their own hands, rather than an opportunity to wait and become sensitive to the Spirit of God. It was the insensitivity of the heart of Saul to the Spirit of God that cost him his kingship. God was looking for a man that would wait upon him, that would desire one thing and one thing alone, "to gaze at His beauty and inquire of Him in the temple" (Psalm 27:4) The Father is looking for five-fold ministry leaders who wait for His leading, and will desire ministries that are born of the Spirit, not man-made religious structures that were created from the flesh.

2. Failing to equip others for the days ahead (1 Samuel 13:22)

"So it came about on the day of battle that neither sword nor spear was found in the hands of any of the people who were with Saul and Jonathan." The mark of a mature church leader is not how many people that they can control, but how many people they can release into ministry.

Church leaders that are headed for Mt. Gilboa build one-man ministries. They see ministry as a means to build up their reputation and status, rather than equipping others for the work of the ministry. Church leaders headed for Mt. Gilboa want to keep the flock spiritually stupid and dependent upon their leadership. They are quick to silence other voices that might influence people and typically smother any move of the Spirit that they themselves did not start.

3. Building Monuments to Themselves (1 Samuel 15:12)

"And Samuel rose early in the morning to meet Saul; and it was told to Samuel, saying, 'Saul came to Carmel, and behold, he set up a monument for himself, then turned and proceeded on down to Gilgal.'"

Church leaders that are headed for Mt. Gilboa build monuments to themselves, rather than monuments to God who enabled them to walk victoriously. These leaders obtain all their rewards upon the earth and will have little, if any, eternal rewards in heaven . These men and women are numbers driven and see salvations and experiences with God as notches on their belts to puff themselves up. They typically answer the question, "How is your ministry doing?" with the response, "We have _____ amount of people attending our services." King Saul saw assignments from the Lord as nothing more than opportunities to make himself look good among the people. He was full of pride and arrogance, and masked it behind being obedient to the Lord.

4. The Need to be Politically Correct (1 Samuel 15:24)

"Then Saul said to Samuel, 'I have sinned; I have indeed transgressed the command of the Lord and your words, because I FEARED THE PEOPLE AND LISTENED TO THEIR VOICE." King Saul was given specific instructions to slaughter the Amalekites, and all they possessed, for what they did to Israel coming out of Egypt. Saul defeated the army, yet spared their King Agag and the choicest of the spoil. King Saul was so blind to his own disobedience that he was at first surprised at Samuel's anger toward his disobedience to the instruction of the Lord. As Samuel delivers a word of judgment to Saul, he finally reveals why he chose to sin; he feared the people and listened to their voice.

Church leaders that are headed for Mt. Gilboa feel that they must be politically correct in any and all situations. Their desire to please the people around them overshadows their need to listen and obey the voice of the Lord. These leaders oftentimes believe that they are walking in the will of the Lord, just as Saul did, because they have been given over to compromise and deception. They are unwilling to slaughter the "Agag's" in the land. These leaders have settled for partial obedience, but do not understand that partial obedience is no obedience at all.

5. Walking in False Humility (1 Samuel 15:30)

"Then Saul said, 'I have sinned; but please honor me now before the elders of my people and before Israel, and go back with me, that I may worship the Lord your God."

Even in King Saul's confession of his sin and

arrogance, he was so full of pride that he sought to be honored amongst the people. Church leaders that are headed for Mt. Gilboa never truly repent of their sins, nor do they make it a public matter. They are full of excuses and are unwilling to submit to the process of restoration, no matter how many years that might take. The high cost of pride is the forfeit of wisdom. Those that walk in false humility will fail time and time again, until their desire to be honored, even in their failures, is uprooted and removed from their lives.

6. The Need to Have a Hand in Everything (1 Samuel 17:38)

"Then Saul clothed David with his garments and put a bronze helmet on his head, and he clothed him with his armor." Young David was the only man in Israel who did not fear Goliath on the day of battle. He took the giant of a man down with one stone and eventually cut his head off, yet King Saul still had a need to have his hand in the battle. By Saul attempting to clothe David in his armor, this was not an act of compassion or concern, this was an attempt to take credit for David's protection on the day of battle. David was wise to throw off the armor and go with what he knew would work; the leading of the Lord.

Church leaders that are headed for Mt. Gilboa simply feel the need to have a hand in every single expression of church and ministry. They demand to know every detail and expect every person to report to them at all times. Their desire to control and manipulate is stifling and exhausting to those around them. These leaders refuse to release people on the day of battle. They must have a hand in other people's successes and victories.

7. Insecurity and Unknown Identity that Fuels Jealousy (1 Samuel 18:8-9)

"Then Saul became very angry, for this saying

displeased him; and he said, 'They have ascribed to David ten thousands, but to me they have ascribed thousands. Now what more can he have but the kingdom. And Saul looked at David with suspicion from that day on."

Church leaders that are headed for Mt. Gilboa look at the successes of those that they are serving as a threat to their leadership. While they voice approval and affirmation to those around them, inwardly they are filled with jealousy. Insecurity and unknown identity are the fuel for why church leaders headed for Mt. Gilboa do not trust others with responsibility, and have the need to take credit for the victories of others.

Can you imagine if young David would have defeated Goliath wearing Saul's armor. As they cheered for David in the streets, Saul would have shouted, "Yes, but he was wearing MY armor!" King Saul was so jealous of the anointing that David walked in that he would spend the rest of his Kingship pursuing David and trying to kill him, rather than pursuing the real enemies of Israel. Church leaders that are headed for Mt. Gilboa spend more time trying to discredit and tear down ministries and people than actually engaging the real enemy, Satan.

The new apostolic generation is going to expose the Kingdom of Saul operating among church leaders, and seek to transition them into a ministry paradigm where they will carry a Davidic heart and spirit that thrives in teamwork, and that loves to train and equip others for the days ahead.

The Kingdom of David

The oasis of Engedi in Israel was known as a hiding place of refuge for young David and his men as he ran for his life from King Saul (1 Samuel 23:29). Although David had already been anointed as King over Israel by the prophet Samuel, he was considered a fugitive by King Saul and his men. It was in a cave in Engedi that David chose, in his words, "not to harm the Lord's anointed" even though he had the opportunity to kill the man who was relentlessly pursuing him for years.

Ultimately, Engedi was the place where David passed a crucial test in his journey toward leading Israel: *he refused to murder King Saul and, therefore, chose not to take his destiny into His own hands.* The reason why God hears the cries that come from Engedi is because the cries from that place are ones that are ultimately surrendered to the Father's will. David even apparently had a prophetic word from the Lord that Saul would be delivered into his hands as his men reminded him, " Behold, this IS the day of which the Lord said to you, 'Behold; I am about to give your enemy into your hand, and you shall do to him as it seems good to you." David was so in tune with the spirit of God in Engedi that he recognized that the prophetic word he received was not so that he could fulfill it by his own hands, but the prophetic word was only meant to test the deepest motives and desires of His heart! Would he take his destiny into his own hands or allow the Lord to further refine and test His heart?

The new apostolic generation will carry the heart of David and be magnetically attracted to leaders who carry this DNA and spirit. Self-promotion is repulsive in the sight of God. It dishonors the grace God wants to give to those who will humble themselves and allow Him to exalt them in due time.

The Seven Signs That Church Leaders Have Been to Engedi

1. They Consistently Refuse the Temptation to

Self-Promote (1 Samuel 24: 17)

"And he said to David, 'You are more righteous than I; for you have dealt well with me, while I have dealt wickedly with you." The very fact that David chose not to take the life of Saul when he was delivered into his hands at Engedi should speak volumes to church leaders everywhere. David recognized that it was only God himself who could promote him, not the works of his own hands.

Church leaders that have been to Engedi do not use ministry to promote themselves, rather they allow the Spirit of God to promote Christ within them. The problem with self-promotion is that it can only be maintained through striving, something David was not willing to do. David recognized that it was God Himself who would establish his kingship, and it would be God Himself who would sustain his kingship. As five-fold ministry is restored to the Church through plurality of eldership, individuals will learn how to prefer, defer, and promote the gifting of those around them, rather than themselves.

2. They Recognize That Only God Can Vindicate Them (1 Samuel 24:10-12)

"Now, my father, see! Indeed, see the edge of your robe in my hand! For in that I cut off the edge of your robe and did not kill you, know and perceive that there is no evil or rebellion in my hands, and I have not sinned against you, though you are lying in wait for my life to take it." It was young David who recognized that only God Himself could clear his name. Taking the life of King Saul would not do it, even though David would have been justified amongst the people in killing Saul.

Church leaders that have been to Engedi allow the Father to be their defender. They do not waste time trying to clear their name or ministry. These leaders are not driven by the praise of men, but rather by the desire to see God get glory in all situations and at all times.

3. They Build Monuments to their Nothingness (I Samuel 24: 14)

"After whom has the king of Israel come out? Whom are you pursuing? A dead dog, a single flea"

Church leaders that have been to Engedi look for opportunities to humble themselves in the midst of difficult circumstances. Wouldn't it have been so easy for young David to grab King Saul in that cave and remind him, before he killed him, of how Samuel the prophet had anointed David king over Israel years before? No, David considered himself a dead dog and a single flea that King Saul was pursuing him. Those that lead and have been to Engedi do not take credit for their success and confess with Paul the Apostle, "What do I possess that I myself have not received?" (1 Corinthians 4:7)

4. They Smell Like Sheep (I Samuel 24:22)

"And Saul went to his home, but David and his men went up to the stronghold." David was just a simple shepherd boy before Samuel anointed his head with oil and proclaimed him King over Israel. Although it would be many years before David took the throne, a shepherd's heart was being developed inside of him from a very young age. David knew the importance of shepherding from within the flock, so it was natural that when he began to be entrusted with a position of leadership, that he knew how to lead from within his own company of men.

Church leaders that have been to Engedi smell like sheep. They do not constantly separate themselves from those that they serve. These church leaders are accessible, and their lives are open books to all and any that ask. Church leaders that have been to Engedi do not treat people like sheep, because they themselves know that they are sheep in need of the Good Shepherd.

5. They are Wilderness Trained (1 Samuel 24:8)

"David bowed with his face to the ground and prostrated himself toward Saul." Here was young David, bowing down before the very man that was trying to kill him! This total act of humility and brokenness was a sheer sign that David was submitted to being wilderness trained.

Church leaders that have been to Engedi understand the difference between the "anointing" and the season of "appointing." They recognize that a "calling" is not a "commissioning." The season of Engedi is evident in the lives of church leaders that have submitted to the process of consecration. David knew the value of being wilderness trained and also realized the destruction that would come if he refused to submit to it. Leaders that have been to Engedi would rather limp into heaven than walk straight into hell.

6. They Strengthen and Encourage Themselves in the Lord (1 Samuel 30:6)

"But David strengthened himself in the Lord his God." The day will come in every church leaders life where there will be no encouragement, no one to offer comfort in some of the greatest times of need. Here David was at Ziklag, absolutely distraught over the Amalekites raiding the Negev where they captured he and his men's families. His own men even began talking of stoning him. David had an important decision to make as a leader. He could either give in to his own fears and give up, or he could turn to the Lord His God and strengthen Himself in who he knew God to be. It was in the wilderness of Engedi that David learned what it meant to be wholeheartedly abandoned to the Lord. Ziklag was simply another test.

Church leaders that have been to Engedi know how to encourage themselves in the Lord. It is what separates them from the lukewarm. Church leaders that have been to

Engedi carry hearts that have been tested by the praise

given to them by men. In less than 24 hours from this

moment in Ziklag, David would be crowned King over

Israel, as Saul and his sons would fall at Mt. Gilboa.

Perhaps David's ability to strengthen and encourage

himself in the Lord was the final test before God Himself

promoted him as King.

7. They Walk in Absolute Obedience (1 Samuel 30:17)

"And David slaughtered them from the twilight until

the evening of the next day; and not a man of them

escaped…" When King Saul was given the assignment to

wipe out the Amalekites and everything they possessed, he

made a choice to spare their King Agag and leave the

choicest of the spoils for Himself and His men. When

David pursued the Amalekites, he slaughtered every last

one that he and his men could get to.

Church leaders that have been to Engedi complete the assignments that God has given them without delay. They understand that partial obedience is no obedience at all. David was tested in Engedi as to whether he would take matters into his own hands by killing Saul, which he refused because he was not released to do so. After inquiring of the Lord at Ziklag, he was released to pursue the Amalekites and slaughter them. Church leaders that have been to Engedi know both when to enter into battle in obedience, and when to leave the battle to the Lord in obedience.

It is vitally important that the new apostolic generation discern and understand what kind of spirit church leaders are operating in. Do they operate in a Saul spirit and are headed to Mt. Gilboa, or do they carry a Davidic dna that will lead them to En gedi? Only church leaders who carry a heart like David will form the new wineskin that God will pour His new wine into upon the earth. Those who carry a Saul Spirit will never commit to plurality of eldership with Jesus Christ being the foundation and cornerstone. Let's now look at the three judgments that fall upon church leaders who build one man ministries.

1. Family Turmoil

The first judgment that God showed me that falls upon church leaders who refuse biblical eldership and accountability is disaster within their own families. The families of five-fold leaders who build one-man ministries have, and will, pay the greatest price for this mistake. Marriage breakdown, and children straying far away from the Lord because dad was working twenty-four seven, are clear indicators that a one-man ministry has been built. God intended the local church burden to be shared among a group of men, not a singular one. I remember sitting with a "senior pastor" of a church whose marriage was failing and all three of his adult children were no longer serving the Lord. He cried in front of me and explained how hard he had worked at the church all his life and so on. He just could not figure out what had happened. I gently leaned in and told him, "Brother, your marriage is failing and your children are no longer serving the Lord because the church has become your mistress and addiction. You seem to be able to fulfill everyone's needs except those who are closest to you."

2. Personal Burnout

The mental picture of one church leader wearing every hat known to man is cause for the personal burnout of thousands upon thousands of church leaders the last 100 years. One man came to me completely exhausted after senior pastoring a small church for over 20 years. I began to teach him about biblical eldership and he wept uncontrollably. He said, "For the last 20 years, I have believed that there must be another way to pastor people." I said, "Yes, it requires you to stop taking the center stage in your church and learn how to work with a team of men who can shepherd the flock together." He said, "That sounds wonderful". I said, "It might sound good, but just remember that you will no longer have control over everything. Your need to solve every problem in the church is the problem." It is common for one-man ministries to suffer from depression, suicidal thoughts, loneliness, no time for hobbies, and even taking prescription pills to deal with the stress and pressures of ministry. These terrible side effects come largely from ministers believing, and being taught, that their job is to be the CEO of their church and everyone will answer to them. Look out! Burnout is inevitable!

3. Moral Failure

Perhaps worst of all is the moral failure that takes place amongst church leaders that is directly related to them building one-man ministries. Whether its stealing money or committing adultery, one-man ministries allow a lack of accountability among church leaders that was never intended by God in the first place. Speaking from personal experience, there is nothing like shepherding the flock of God with a team of elders who all hold one another accountable and walk in fellowship as brothers. It is near impossible, if true and intimate relationship is forged among a team of elders who shepherd the flock of God together, for there to be moral failure, or for it at least to not be caught in its infant stage. Biblical eldership provides a system of checks and balances that one-man ministries so desperately need!

How many thousands of lives have been ruined or damaged in America and the nations of the earth in just the last 30 years, because one man or woman decided that they were going to build an entire ministry surrounded by what they, and they alone, can offer the people? I believe much of the destruction that we have seen in the American church has been a result of reaping what we have sown. We have sown and established unbiblical patterns and systems of government for church leaders, and have reaped the judgments of God because of it. May we repent, learn from our mistakes, and confess our need for one another! We must return back to the Scriptures in order to understand how to build the house of God.

Loving One-Man Ministries

I would be remiss to not address an outstanding issue regarding this subject and it's simply this: people love and adore one-man ministries. Just as they cried out for a king in Israel, so the global Church has cried out for gifted men and women whom they can follow and put their trust in. We build entire church empires off of the gifting of singular men and women, and when they inevitably retire, or fall, we see traumatic fallouts every single time.

Attempting to establish a team of elders who work together in the shepherding of a local church is the single hardest thing God has ever asked me to do. To refuse to put one man in absolute authority, and allow him to cast the sole vision and direction of the church, has been a tremendous challenge. Building the house of God according to how He designed it requires the insecurity, jealousy, control, and pride of men to be absolutely crucified. Not only is it difficult learning how to work together with a team of leaders in establishing a vision and shepherding the flock of God, but the people that come and attend will continually cry out for one man to do everything. Most church-goers want one man to do everything. They are looking for a golden spoon, a man that they can worship and trust, when God never intended this to be!

Church Hurt

The term, "I've been hurt by the church" has become an epidemic in the global Church. Do you know why so many people have been hurt by the church? The answer is because the church is not being built and established according to the New Testament pattern. By choosing to build one-man ministries, we are actually setting the people of God up for total failure and disappointment. They have been taught to depend upon a single man for their every need, when they should be redirected to a team of elders who can provide oversight that instructs them that, ultimately, Jesus the Good Shepherd is their source and guide in life.

Church Addiction

If establishing a plurality of elders to govern the local church and putting an end to one-man ministries was easy to implement, we would see it all around us. Although it is woven throughout the books of Acts and the Epistles, it is scarce these days. But why? I believe the answer is revealed and dates back to the very first king of Israel, King Saul. His life and time upon the throne revealed that he was insecure, full of pride and jealousy, and found his identity in what he did, not who he was.

It is church leaders who are addicted to the praise of men and carry insecurity, pride, and jealousy for others that will radically oppose plurality of eldership and, consequently, model their ministries after the kingdom of

Saul. In the spirit of David, I see a new apostolic generation who will restore Jesus Christ as the foundation and head of His Church. Five-fold ministry leaders working together to train and equip the saints in a spirit of humility will literally change the landscape of the global church. No longer will men build their own kingdoms, but rather they will unite to establish the kingdom of God upon the earth. Behold, there is a new wineskin forming in the earth that holds the key to massive reformation in the days ahead. Let's take a closer look at the new wineskin in the next chapter!

-4-
The New Wineskin is Forming

With the rise of the new apostolic generation in the earth, a new wineskin is forming in the body of Christ that will hold the new wine God is pouring out. A major part of the new wineskin is simply the global Church returning back to biblical foundation. In other words, the "new" that God is bringing to the body of Christ in this hour is simply a restoration of what has been lost, and even forfeited, over time. We have sadly lost Jesus Christ as the foundation, cornerstone, and head of the Church, therefore God is raising up a new apostolic generation that will carry the grace to restore Him back to His rightful place.

Apostolic ministry carries specific grace to reveal and uncover Jesus Christ to His people. Because much of the contemporary Church has chosen to build upon faulty foundations, such as the personality and charisma of men, a confrontation and tension is being released across the global body of Christ. While some are claiming to be of "Cephas" and others "Apollos" (well known leaders in the body of Christ), God is releasing a new apostolic generation that will tear down and expose these personality cults, and call the body to get connected back to its true foundation, cornerstone, source, and head - Jesus Christ. The enemy of the new apostolic generation is the spirit of religion, which is man worship.

The Platform Idol

I'm convinced that church leaders who always want the microphone and refuse to get off a stage, to learn how to actively mother and father the current generations in the church, will become obsolete in the days ahead. Obsolete meaning: out of date, churches shutting down, no longer effective, and bearing little to no fruit type of obsolete.

The "old wineskin" in the Church is currently trembling because the new apostolic generation is tired of the 'one-man-ministry-does-all' model. This apostolic company is pregnant with a vision of reformation in the global Church that is built on team ministry. They are looking for fathers and mothers who are willing to roll up their sleeves and do life with them. They don't care much about the polished sermons anymore. They are actually looking for church leaders to model a healthy marriage, and what it looks like for kids to serve the Lord with everything in them.

The "old wineskin" in the Church is confused because the new apostolic generation can see through and recognize "fake" more than ever before. The days of plastic smiles and worshipping "platform ministry" are over. The "living room" in people's homes is now becoming the main attraction and focus. The new apostolic generation will be taught and learn how to steward the presence of God in their homes before they ever try to welcome Him in a church service.

My heart aches and groans for so many church leaders (especially those in their 50's and 60's) that are set on continuing to do a model of church that has become obsolete. It worked back in the day, but those days are over. I continue to meet church leaders across the United States and the world who are completely disconnected from the hunger rising in the body of Christ. As one national church leader in his early 60's recently told me, "The problem with the current hunger in this generation is that they want intimate relationship, which requires too much out of church leaders. In my day, the people were satisfied with coming and watching us minister. Now the people actually want to get involved, it's too bad."

As someone who ministers around the USA and the world frequently, and interacts with hundreds of church leaders every year, I can assure you that this is NOT an isolated incident. I'm prophesying to you that thousands of church leaders in the global Church are on the ropes, not sure if they can even keep going, because they have failed to recognize the new wineskin that is forming in the Church. The church leaders in the days ahead who will form the new wineskin that God will pour the new wine into (whether they be 25 or 65 years old) will model and teach the following:

1. Give up the Microphone.

2. The Stage is not to be Idolized.

3. Fire the Armor Bearers and Entourage.

4. Stop Hiding in the Green Room.

5. Be Accessible and Available to the People.

6. Don't ask the saints to do anything you wouldn't do.

7. Father and Mother through Discipling.

8. Be Real and Transparent. Share the Mistakes.

9. Value the Prayer Room over the Platform.

10. Don't Compromise the Word of God.

11. Invite Saints into your Home and Lifestyle.

12. Empower and Make Room for Others to Lead.

13. Train, Equip, and Release.

14. Multiplication and Legacy are the Standard.

15. Humility brings Honor and Pride Repels Saints.

As these fifteen strategies are prayerfully considered by church leaders across the earth, they will pave the way for Jesus Christ to take center stage in the Church. The new apostolic generation will be fathered and mothered by leaders who desire to walk among them, not talk down to them. The primary resisters and persecutors of the new apostolic generation will be church leaders and apostles who would rather build their own kingdoms and networks, rather than live to see Jesus Christ glorified in all things. This old wineskin of building ministries and churches off of men and their gifting will not appeal to the new apostolic generation emerging. There is a new wineskin forming in the earth filled with fathering and mothering behind the scenes.

Fathering the New Wineskin

I'm convinced that one of the most difficult things for the new apostolic generation to accept is the fact that they will be fathered and mothered by no named saints who cannot offer them platforms and stages. God spoke to me and said, "I'm raising up a well-known new apostolic generation of leaders and will give them no-name fathers and mothers, so that MY NAME will be recognized and remembered in the earth." Much of the spiritual sickness and disease involved in apostolic ministry in the earth today is born from what I call "opportunistic relationships". In other words, we have way too many young people wanting to connect with fathers and mothers simply based off of what kind of platforms and invitations these leaders can give them. I believe many of the gifted leaders in the new apostolic generation will be fathered and mothered by individuals that can offer them nothing but deep affection, comfort, correction, and serious prayer and intercession, which are the very things they so desperately need.

Here come the Firebrands

To church leaders that walk in insecurity and jealousy, the new apostolic generation that carries zeal and passion for Jesus Christ and the advancement of His kingdom will look like rebellious and prideful people.

In an open vision, I saw the spirit of Saul (insecurity

and jealousy) operating through church leaders that will attempt to assassinate the new apostolic generation who are crazy about the presence of Jesus and absolutely love prayer, worship, and the place of encounter. This emerging apostolic company does not care who is preaching or leading, so long as God manifests His glory.

I feel deeply compelled by the Spirit of God to speak a father's blessing as a leader in the body of Christ over the new apostolic generation that understands that the current wineskin of the global Church cannot contain the new wine God is pouring out. I declare, "You are not rebellious or prideful because you know there has to be more than church programs, three songs, and a nice motivational sermonette. Your concern over many church leaders who have lost the fresh anointing of the Holy Spirit because they have forgotten their first love is justified!

Even as your heart has longed to be fathered and

given permission to burn for Jesus, do not allow an orphan heart and a spirit of bitterness to grab a hold of your heart. Yes, you are hurting and feel rejection, but as you walk in humility and allow God to heal you, He will use you in the days ahead to do that for those you lead which your fathers refused to do for you."

Much of the new apostolic generation emerging has not been fathered and released like they should have because of the jealousy and insecurity of their leaders, but in the days ahead, they will move in an opposite spirit! Because they were constricted and oppressed, when they lead, they will release and empower. Because all they knew were leaders who lost the fresh anointing of the Holy Spirit, they will walk in intimacy and a spirit of prayer. They will continually lift up the name of Jesus and seek to root and ground this generation in the Word of God.

I'm absolutely convinced that an old wineskin of church leaders and apostles who crave the platform, influence, and money is being prophetically exposed in this hour, and the new apostolic generation is being called forth who will walk in humility, healing, and honor toward those who have hurt them.

The Apostolic Shift

Through prayer and seeking God, I believe the new apostolic generation is pursuing Jesus Christ at such an accelerated pace right now that they can't currently find a spiritual father/mother that understands them within a hundred miles of where they live if they tried. Some of them can't even find a church in their entire city that's fiery in the place of prayer, embracing five-fold ministry teams, and building upon the rock solid foundation of Jesus Christ. A great number of the new apostolic generation is surrounded by business-as-usual models of church in their current towns and cities, and church leaders who treat their calling like a nine-to-five job.

The fire and passion for Jesus Christ that the new apostolic generation carries continually exposes the dryness of the religion around them. These apostolic messengers have caught, and are currently catching hold of, the revelation that their radical fire can only be stewarded by radical accountability.

In the spirit realm, I am beginning to see desperation manifest in the hearts of the new apostolic generation, as many of them are literally going to quit their jobs and move halfway across their country, simply to connect with a spiritual mother/father that is running after God with all their might. They are asking themselves, "Where are the spiritual leaders who are consumed with Jesus Christ and establishing His kingdom upon the earth? Where are the mothers and fathers calling the prayer meetings and actually attending and leading them?"

Ultimately, the new apostolic generation is searching for secure fathers/mothers that will give them permission to burn for Christ, and offer loving correction and discipleship where needed. These apostolic messengers are not rebellious or prideful, they are just desperate for more of Jesus and will pay any price to encounter Him in more intimate ways. I believe that because what I am saying is true, we will begin to see two realities manifest in the global body of Christ:

1. Increased tension between the new apostolic generation and religious leaders who do not understand their fire and passion. The new apostolic generation will constantly be wrongly labeled rebellious and prideful by those walking in a Saul spirit of insecurity and jealousy who are building monuments to themselves. I see great

wounding and pain being inflicted upon the new apostolic generation as they are destined to have the scars of religion, but the healing balm of God the Father upon them.

2. Where there are spiritual mothers/fathers (regardless of their age), that are centered upon Jesus Christ and desire to build His kingdom and not their own, they will attract the new apostolic generation from the four corners of the earth because they will give other's permission to burn, not stomp out their fire. To those who are ready to father/mother and stoke the fire of this emerging apostolic company, you will have your hands full in the best of ways!

People Will Attack You

The new apostolic generation must be warned that they cannot do the will of God without challenging the way things have always been, and without causing catalytic changes in the body of Christ. This will inevitably cause the old wineskin of church leaders and apostles to stumble, scoff, criticize, and falsely accuse them.

There is a demonic strategy set up against the new apostolic generation that is not only aimed at destroying them, but also scattering the followers. If Satan's attack is successful, everyone involved will come out of the battle hurt and wounded. Remember, Satan uses people to attack, criticize, and question apostolic pioneers so that those who are getting set free, refreshed, and empowered by their life and ministry will become confused, disoriented, and altogether stop listening to the new apostolic generation.

A Prophetic Warning to the New Apostolic Generation

God would say to this emerging apostolic company, "You cannot allow yourself to become so easily manipulated by people's criticisms and attacks. Do not try to maintain peace in your heart and life based off of whether people accept or reject you." Most of the time God will not deliver you from your accusers, but rather He will actually save you by killing the part of you that is vulnerable to the devil by using the accusations themselves.

As the new apostolic generation, you must recognize that both God and the devil want you to die, but for different reasons. Satan wants to destroy you through attacks and criticisms, and then drain you by your unwavering need to explain yourself and your side of the story. (Please stop wasting your time and energy doing this!) On the other hand, God wants to crucify that part in you that was so easily exploited by the devil to begin with. The rest and peace that you are so desiring in your life and ministry will only come when you finally die to what people say and think about you.

New Apostolic Generation, in order to deliver you from the praise of men, God will baptize you in their criticisms and attacks. It is painful. You will lose many friendships along the way and the misunderstanding will be many. You will pay a price that most around you will never see nor understand. You are speaking a language of reform and awakening that many in the body of Christ just don't have an eye or ear for yet. Do not grow discouraged and, most of all, do not be surprised when the attacks and criticisms come. Rather than rushing to defend or explain yourself, my advice would be to go before the Lord and ask Him, "What inside of me are you exposing through the accusation and attacks of others that needs to die?"

The Days Ahead

The new apostolic generation will have a difficult

journey of learning how to honor and walk in humility toward those who have labored in previous generations, but also be faithful to the revelation and assignments God has given them. I believe that there are thousands of mothers and fathers in the earth right now that are ready to receive this emerging apostolic company. These seasoned spiritual parents might not be famous or have the ability to open up doors of opportunity, but they will love, faithfully pray, and speak the truth when necessary.

I also believe that there are thousands of mothers and fathers in the earth right now who are operating under an old wineskin of platform ministry built on insecurity, pride, and jealousy that will absolutely loathe the new apostolic generation. As these emerging apostolic reformers and pioneers begin to restore Jesus Christ back as the foundation, cornerstone, and head of His Church, and cry out for plurality of eldership that welcomes the five-fold ministry, they will be fiercely opposed and persecuted by many church leaders who are building their own kingdoms and ministries.

The Example of David

Killing Goliath was both the BEST and WORST event that ever happened to young David! (1 Samuel 17) For the new apostolic generation, that big open door, that promotion, that spotlight, that book signing, that revival, that tv interview could unleash the greatest jealousy, insecurity, and strife from fathers/mothers and brothers/sisters that some have ever known, but will also set the stage for them to fulfill your destiny in the earth.

A generation of fathers (Saul) could only celebrate David so long as he would wear his armor. Once David became more successful than Saul by killing Goliath and defeating the Philistines, his jealousy would hunt David the rest of his life.

For the new apostolic generation, some of those fathers/mothers that once cheered you on in your earlier years when you were in their shadow, will despise you, slander you, and try to kill your influence as you surpass them in anointing and grace. Their words will sting you, try to poison and confuse you, and derail you from pursuing God with all your might!

A generation of peers (Eliab and Abinadab) could only see David as their baby brother, and the insignificant one who tended to the little sheep. Once David knew he was ready to cut the head off Goliath, and he did, the jealousy and insecurity of David's brothers soared!

For the new apostolic generation, some of those brothers/sisters you once ran with, and were even constantly overlooked with because of their talents and skills, will writhe in anger, jealousy, and insecurity as they watch you fulfill your destiny. They will stir up gossip, slander, and false accusation among brothers/sisters around your own age, simply because they cannot stand that God chose you to fulfill this assignment and not them!

To the new apostolic generation, I say: keep praying, keep dreaming, and keep pressing, but do not disregard this prophetic warning of the days that lie ahead of you! Count the cost. Recognize the spiritual warfare that is about to be unleashed against you and yours. You will lose some good fathers and mothers who once encouraged you as a rookie, but who will not be able to stand you as an emerging pioneer. Pray for them and honor them the best you know how. They just can't see you the way God sees you. Don't become distracted or disappointed with the Eliab's and Abinadab's (brothers and sisters) around you. They once ran with you and spoke well of you, but now their insecurity will cause them to want to see your downfall. When they spread rumors about you, choose to speak good of them. God will bless you for it.

Finally new apostolic generation, be warned, but also be encouraged! Your Jonathan's are coming to your rescue! You maybe once had fathers/mothers that no longer pour into you, and maybe even brothers/sisters that you were once close with, but a company of Jonathan's is quickly coming to your side! They will get you and the assignment on your life without questions. They are willing to run with you, but really they just want to be your friend! As you emerge, grow in your calling, and navigate the wilderness, they will be with you every step of the way.

-5-
The New Apostolic Generation

While on an extended fast in November of 2016, I had an encounter with God late one night that shook me to my core. The weighty glory of His presence filled my home as He spoke to me and said, "Of all the five ministries functioning in the body of Christ, (apostles, prophets, teachers, pastors, and evangelists) the greatest level of deception is operating in apostolic ministry. There is coming an increasing polarization to this specific ministry. On the one hand, you will witness true apostles rise who walk in authentic apostolic ministry, but on the other hand, you will see false apostles rise who will spread soulish and false apostolic ministry to the ends of the earth."

I began to weep as I tangibly felt the grief of God

come over me in a way that I had never experienced before. I cried out and said, "Father, what is the deception that you speak of that is operating in the apostolic movement?" The Holy Spirit immediately quoted 2 Corinthians 11:3 back to me, "But I am afraid lest as the serpent deceived Eve by his craftiness, your minds should be led astray from the simplicity and purity of devotion to Christ." I started wailing even harder. I heard the voice of God speak again to me and say, "Jeremiah, I am raising up a new apostolic generation in the earth that will restore pure and simple hearted devotion to My Son Jesus Christ once again. They will expose a false wineskin of apostolic ministry in the earth that is seeking to exalt men and their ministries above My great name. Their greed for money, influence, control, and their hunger for pre-eminence in all things will be confronted. I'm sounding the alarm now for my Son is returning quickly. I am about to pour out My

Spirit upon the new apostolic generation without measure as they testify of My Son Jesus Christ."

It is out of this word from the Lord and encounter with Him that my heart has been burdened beyond measure concerning apostolic ministry in the earth. With the increasing polarization that is coming in the apostolic movement, it is very urgent and necessary to call forth the new apostolic generation and to warn the body of Christ of a false apostolic movement that will desire pre-eminence, influence, money, and titles. With sobriety, we must seek to establish a biblical foundation for authentic apostolic ministry, while also exposing the soulish and false practices among the apostolic movement.

I see a new apostolic generation rising in the earth today who are radically Jesus Christ centered. In fact, I'm convinced that the primary earmark of authentic apostolic ministry is a revelation and fresh experience of the person of Jesus Christ. I believe that God has specifically given apostles the grace to connect the body to its true head, Jesus Christ. Without healthy and biblical apostolic ministry functioning in the body, we cannot know the mind of Christ and walk in a spirit of revelation like we ought to.

A Revelation of Jesus Christ

As Paul penned the Epistles, he always began by referring to himself as, "Paul, an apostle of Jesus Christ." Notice how Paul did not refer to himself as an apostle of spiritual warfare, deliverance, wealth, spiritual gifts or any other subject. While apostles may carry grace and revelation concerning certain subjects in the kingdom of God, Paul was emphatic that he was an apostle of Jesus Christ who had an encounter and growing revelation of the Son of God. Regarding his accolades and accomplishments in life, Paul was quick to consider all of them a loss in view of the surpassing value of knowing Christ Jesus his Lord. (Phil 3:8) As a called apostle, Paul was "Christ centered" not "Christian subjects-centered." Not only did he give his life and ministry to revealing and manifesting Jesus Christ to His body, but he always introduced himself as "Paul, an apostle of Jesus Christ". Never did he introduce himself as "Apostle Paul" one time in Scripture. Why is this so important? Because Paul knew how to distinguish his identity from his function. Paul's identity was a son to the Father, but his function was that of an apostle called by Jesus Christ. When apostles wrap their identity in their function and make them one and the same, they will make the mistake of exalting themselves and their ministries above the glorious person of Jesus Christ every single time. True apostolic grace is recognized, not demanded. If so called "apostles" have to demand or require that others call them by a title, then this is an

immediate red flag that cannot be disregarded.

The Example of Paul

Paul was the premier church planter, itinerant

minister, and apostolic father in/to his generation.

Pioneering the path, hundreds and perhaps thousands of

messengers would soon follow in his footsteps and attempt

to model the blueprints He had received out of a revelation

of and encounter with Jesus Christ (Gal 1:12).

As Paul traveled the world and rubbed shoulders

with other men and women who were supposedly carrying

out his same mission, he laments and profoundly writes in

Philippians 2:20-22 and says, "For I have NO ONE ELSE

of kindred spirit who will genuinely be concerned for your

welfare. For they all seek after THEIR OWN interests,

NOT those of Christ Jesus. But you know of Timothy's

proven worth, that he served with me in the furtherance of the gospel like a child serving his father."

What a startling and shocking lamentation from Paul the Apostle! In his day where hundreds and perhaps thousands of messengers had "traveling ministries" and claimed to be "apostles", he could find only ONE MAN, his spiritual son Timothy, who carried his same heart and passion for seeing Jesus Christ exalted and not personal agendas and ministries.

In the earth today, would Paul make the same shocking lament concerning all our "traveling ministries" and "apostles"? Would he dare say that he could hardly find any itinerant preachers and apostles who are actually promoting Jesus Christ and His Kingdom, and not their own selfish agendas? Furthermore, what if the bond between spiritual sons/daughters and fathers was not that they had similar preaching styles and lingo, but that they actually only desired Jesus Christ to get all the glory?

The New Apostolic Generation Rising

God is raising up a new apostolic generation in the earth who will actually preach "Christ" out of a personal encounter and revelation of who He really is. When these anointed vessels enter into cities and churches, the saints will actually become convinced that these apostles are more concerned about their maturity in Christ, than they are about picking up another honorarium check and blowing in and out of another city. This apostolic company is going to live in continual birth pains until Christ is formed in those God has called them to influence. (Gal 4:19) The new apostolic generation emerging will proclaim Jesus Christ and all of His glory. The Holy Spirit will anoint their declarations and restore fascination and love for the Son of God as they minister.

The new apostolic generation will help usher in revival to the Church centered upon the knowledge of God and encountering the person of Jesus. This apostolic company of burning and shining lamps will devour the Word of God. They will say "yes" to fresh encounters on the road to Emmaus, where the unveiling of Christ will be made known to them through the Law, the Psalms, the Prophets, and the New Testament. God's eternal purpose in Christ Jesus shall be manifested to this generation through these apostolic voices.

Apostolic ministry that does not recognize that to gain revelation concerning Christ is everything, and to forfeit it is futile, is not authentic apostolic ministry. The primary calling of the new apostolic generation is to unveil the glorious person of Jesus Christ to His body. (Col 1:17; Eph. 3:8-11) The new apostolic generation has been commissioned by the Father Himself to uncover and reveal

Jesus Christ as the foundation, the cornerstone, and head of the Church. The new apostolic generation will consistently teach, preach, and prophesy on the life, death, burial, resurrection, ascension, and second coming of Jesus Christ. Jesus Himself will be their central focus and message.

Ten Earmarks of The New Apostolic Generation

In order for the body of Christ to recognize this new apostolic generation centered on Jesus, there must be a profile developed and earmarks established, for the body to receive them in our midst. Here are ten earmarks of the new apostolic generation:

1. The New Apostolic Generation is Centered on Christ

The Greek verb for apostle is "apostello" which means, "to send forth with a divine commission." Christopher Johnson says that, "an interpretive meaning of the term "apostle" is: "one who has been sent forth with a specific, divine commission, TO REPRESENT THE ONE who has commissioned them." (The Fullness of Ministry, Fishnet Publications 2015 page 127) The new apostolic generation will have no interest in representing themselves and their ministries to the public. They will be sent into regions and territories to represent Jesus Christ. (Phil 2:20-22)

2. The New Apostolic Generation is Called by Christ

In Galatians 1, Paul explains with clarity how he was called by JESUS CHRIST to be an apostle. He received the gospel through a revelation of JESUS CHRIST (v.12). He goes on to say, "God was pleased to REVEAL HIS SON IN ME..." (Galatians 1:16) He didn't choose to be an "apostle" because he thought it was cool and popular. God chose Paul so that He might show him how much he would have to SUFFER for His Name. (Acts

9:16) The new apostolic generation has been called by Jesus Himself through radical encounters and authentic testimony. They will not boast in their ordination or accolades, but testify of the One who called them by divine appointment. These apostolic messengers do not self-promote, but rather the endorsement of heaven is upon their lives and ministries.

3. The New Apostolic Generation Builds on Christ

The new apostolic generation will not build upon any other foundation than JESUS CHRIST. To "align" with this generation is to submit oneself to a radical pursuit of a revelation of Jesus Christ. True apostles will not, and do not, plant and build churches and ministries upon themselves or their ministry gifts, rather they plant churches upon a revelation of Jesus Christ. The new apostolic generation will seek to remove any unnecessary attention off of themselves in the planting of churches and ministries. We will see churches and ministries planted by the new apostolic generation built on Christ and Christ alone.

4. The New Apostolic Generation Preaches Christ

Paul continues to explain his apostolic calling in Galatians 1:16 as he says, "God was pleased to reveal His Son in me, that I might PREACH HIM among the Gentiles…" He proclaimed to the Corinthians that "I have resolved to know nothing but JESUS CHRIST and Him crucified." (1 Cor 2:2). To the church at Philippi, he said, "I count all things to be a loss in view of the surpassing value of knowing JESUS CHRIST MY LORD." (Philippians 3:8) True apostles continually preach JESUS CHRIST. True apostolic preaching is the preaching of JESUS CHRIST. The new apostolic generation will constantly preach on the life, death, burial, resurrection, ascension, and second coming of Jesus Christ. When these apostolic messengers finish teaching and preaching in regions and cities, the worship and exaltation of Jesus Christ will explode in the hearts of sinners and saints alike.

5. The New Apostolic Generation Manifests Christ

The new apostolic generation will manifest JESUS CHRIST in the earth through extraordinary acts of humility and meekness. This apostolic company will not be title-oriented. They have no need for public recognition; only that Jesus Christ Himself receives all the glory and the praise. The new apostolic generation will take the true authority that they have been given and manifest the gentleness and humility of Jesus Christ. (Matthew 11:29) Apostles are foot washers and bondservants. (1 Cor 4:9-14) They do not parade around with entourages and armor bearers.

6. The New Apostolic Generation are Fools for Christ

The new apostolic generation will be mocked and

slandered. While they will be loved and cherished by some, many will reject and falsely accuse them incessantly. When they preach Christ, there will either be revival or riot. They will declare with Paul, "We are fool's for Christ's sake, we are weak, we are without honor, we are hungry, we are thirsty, we are poorly clothed, we are roughly treated, we toil with our own hands". (1 Cor 4:10-11) The old guard of apostles, who have built their ministries on platform titles, will despise and persecute the new apostolic generation because of the humility and meekness they walk in.

7. The New Apostolic Generation are Reviled for Christ

The new apostolic generation will be reviled and continually asked to endure for the sake of Christ. Their focus on Jesus Christ will continually cause them to be despised by others who would rather emphasize other subjects in the kingdom of God. These apostolic messengers will be consumed with laying Jesus Christ as the foundation and cornerstone of the Church, and the religious spirit hates this pursuit. True apostles are continually rejected because they will not build on any other foundation than Jesus Christ. (Eph 2:20, 1 Cor 4:13)

8. The New Apostolic Generation are Fathers in Christ

The new apostolic generation will carry and possess the Father heart of God for His children. They will teach and know experientially the power of the Fatherhood of God. Fatherhood is at the center of authentic apostleship. The new apostolic generation will not father according to their own desires, but they will father IN CHRIST JESUS. As Paul stated, "IN CHRIST JESUS, I have become your father" (1 Cor 4:15). The life source of true apostles who father sons and daughters is JESUS CHRIST! Finding young people that can do your bidding, and then calling yourself an apostle, is not fathering. True apostolic fathering is focused upon the person and work of Jesus Christ.

9. The New Apostolic Generation are Miracle Workers for Christ

The new apostolic generation will minister in signs, wonders, and miracles. They will be a supernatural people. As Paul said, "Truly the signs of an apostle were wrought among you in all patience, in signs, and wonders, and mighty deeds" (2 Cor 12:11-12). The new apostolic generation will carry authority over demons, principalities, sickness, and disease. If there are no consistent miracles when they minister, they are not true apostles.

10. The New Apostolic Generation Possesses the Character of Christ

The new apostolic generation will carry the DNA of Jesus Christ inside their heart and ministry. They understand that in order to be first, they must be last. They recognize that in order to be the greatest, they have to get in the back of the line. True apostles embrace the upside down kingdom that Jesus Christ taught. In the words of Paul, "we (apostles) are the scum of the world" (1 Cor 4:13). The new apostolic generation will be filled with the fruit of the Holy Spirit and will not be prideful, arrogant, and lovers of money. These apostolic messengers do not itch the ears of the carnal, but rather preach the truth in love.

God is releasing a new apostolic generation to the Church who are absolutely possessed, captivated, and fascinated with the person and work of Jesus Christ. Their emergence will stir and call for mass repentance among those who are claiming to be "apostles" in the body of Christ and are not. The soulish and false apostolic movement that is building their kingdoms and ministries will come under strong conviction, as they recognize how far they have fallen from pure and simple devotion to Jesus.

The global body of our Lord is about to have a massive wake up call concerning how disconnected we have become from our head Jesus Christ, and the new apostolic generation is going to pioneer this awakening.

-6-
Apostolic Fathering

The new apostolic generation will restore and recover true apostolic fathering to the body of Christ. The need for saints and church leadership to transition out of religious denominational covering, to truly being apostolically fathered, has never been greater. As someone who travels around the United States and the world preaching in over thirty five churches and conferences a year, less than ten percent of church leaders that I minister for have a spiritual father and are actively being instructed, corrected, and encouraged on a weekly basis.

The percentage drops even lower when you ask believers if they are being spiritually fathered. It is a heartbreaking epidemic, to say the least. Meanwhile, the saints cry out for church leaders to be their spiritual fathers when church leaders themselves are not being spiritually fathered. Sure, they are part of a denominational covering, but they are lacking an intimate, vulnerable, and fathering relationship with an older man in the faith. We must cry out for this to change. When church leaders refuse to be fathered, the church becomes an orphanage run by orphans, and the orphan spirit wreaks havoc in a generation.

The True Apostles are Rising Up

It is imperative that the new apostolic generation identifies who the true apostolic fathers are, so that they can discern any form of counterfeit. Remember, God said that the "greatest deception of all five ministries is operating in apostolic ministry". A true apostle is always thinking of you, praying for you, and longing to see you with the affection of Jesus Christ. Their heart is with you!

They are joyful over you, and at the same time, deeply burdened for you concerning your growth in Christ (Gal 4:19; Phil 1:8; Col 1:9).

For three years in Ephesus, Paul never ceased personally warning and exhorting the elders of the church, night and day, and with tears (Acts 20:31). And when he met them at Miletus to bid them a final farewell, "They all WEPT as they embraced and kissed him..." (Acts 20:37-38). They loved Paul and knew him to be a true father who loved them. This is what apostolic fatherhood is all about saints. We must stop settling for cheap networking schemes and marketing traps in the global Church to satisfy the ache in this generation for true apostolic fathering.

Do you claim to have an apostle? When is the last time they wept over you, as you felt their Father's heart for you deep down inside your spirit? I know people claiming to have an "apostle" who can hardly get a phone call with them, or one meeting every three months. But they do pay a monthly "fee" to rent their "apostles" name so they can feel safe and "covered".

Do you claim to be an apostle? Are you just collecting people's money and building your network, or are you actually involved in authentic relationship with your sons and daughters, and praying for them night and day? In fact, there are some apostles that travel so much, and blow in and out of every city that, the truth is, it's impossible for them to truly father anyone because they just don't have the time or energy.

I'm convinced that true apostolic fatherhood is going to be restored in this generation. Fathers investing into sons and daughters for FREE, because it's their delight and highest privilege in life. There will be apostolic fathers choosing not to travel so much, because they realize they will have a far greater impact staying home and discipling the next generation, rather than blowing in and out of the next conference to make a quick buck.

There will be apostolic fathers who will be accessible and will model for the next generation what a great marriage and child rearing should look like. There is a tremendous reformation that is coming to the apostolic movement, but it will only come through uprooting and tearing down carnality and deception before the building and the planting can take place. It's going to be a challenge, but true apostolic fathers were made for this. Now is the time for the true apostles to arise and walk in authentic apostolic fatherhood.

Apostles Know it is Better to Give than Receive

As previously mentioned, Paul the Apostle ministered to the body and Elders at Ephesus for a period of more than three years. As an apostolic voice and father in their lives, he shares his heart and motives with them in a crystal clear way when he says, "I have not coveted anyone's silver or gold or clothing. You yourselves know that these hands of mine have supplied my own needs and the needs of my companions. In everything I did, I showed you that by this kind of hard work we must help the weak…" (Acts 20:33-35)

As a called apostle, Paul had no desire to be a financial burden to the saints there. He labored among them in the marketplace and set a powerful example for other called apostles throughout the ages. Seeking to explain his actions, he reminded the leaders that, "we must help the weak" and the words of the Lord Jesus Christ, "it is better to give than receive". (v.35)

How does Paul's heart and passion for apostolic ministry in Ephesus compare to current apostolic trends in the earth that charge fees and require specific honorariums to come minister? Why do many so called "modern day apostles" demand to be treated like a Hollywood celebrity, operating in a spirit of greed and mammon, and act like it's all Scriptural? The Spirit of God wants to make this clear, because many of them are not apostles, and are acting like scam artists who push their pyramid scams in order to get rich quick. For a so called "apostle" to require specific honorariums to come preach, and to charge saints certain "fees" to be a part of a network, is nothing more than Babylonian harlotry.

I'm convinced that some of those claiming to be "apostles" and running "apostolic networks" in the body of Christ, are really just business-type CEO's who need to take their manipulation, charisma, and lust for power and money somewhere else. They need to go sell their products and schemes to the world, and stop defiling authentic

Christ-centered apostolic ministry.

We are going to see the rise of true apostles in this generation who recognize that it is better to give than receive. These fathers will give all they have away, free of charge, and consider it an honor and privilege to share and impart the portion of Christ that God has given them to this next generation. We must not be surprised when the names of these authentic apostles are not recognized by the public, but known by their Father in heaven.

The Apostolic Networking Merry-go-round

In 1 Thessalonians 2:5-12, Paul writes concerning five specific earmarks of apostolic ministry. They are as follows: 1. Apostles do not lord their authority over the saints, but rather they minister in gentleness as a nursing mother tenderly cares for her own children.

2. Apostles are not greedy and do not desire to be a

financial burden to those to whom they minister. 3. Apostles are fathers who exhort, encourage, and challenge the saints to walk in a manner worthy of God's call on their life. 4. Apostles do not come to flatter saints with their words, nor do they seek glory and praise from men. 5. Apostles are full of fond affection for the saints, and impart life and love through relationship, not networking or hierarchy.

In a season of intense prayer and fasting concerning apostolic ministry in the earth, I received a prophetic dream where God said to me, "My people must be warned of the coming apostolic merry-go-round. In the days of Paul some claimed to be of Cephas and others Apollos, yet it is no different in the days that you are living in. False allegiance to man is what has caused the immaturity of much of the apostolic ministry in the earth."

We are living in a day/age, in which, in order to be a

spiritual son or daughter to many so-called apostles, one must pay their monthly dues, or be labeled "false sons and daughters." In other words, these charlatans are asking people to rent their name per month so that they can declare that they are operating under "apostolic covering and authority." Through fear, intimidation, and control, the apostolic networking merry-go-round is being established and advanced in the earth. In a gifted generation that is hungering for fathering, they are being prostituted and pimped and don't even know it. If anyone dares to challenge these so-called apostles, they will be blacklisted, and the minions working in these networks will be told not to associate with these individuals. A secret society is being formed within these networks that more resembles the mob, rather than the bride of Christ.

Unfortunately, in order to preserve their public image and reputation, these "apostles" will only network with certain individuals from whom they can benefit. It's all about money, applause, and public image. I'm convinced, many of these con artists posing as apostles need to go open up a business in the world, and stop bringing their greed and filth into the body of Christ. They are using and abusing the saints as they fill up their travel itinerary and boast about how many leaders are submitted to them. It's disgusting in the sight of God.

The problem with some of the apostolic networking in the earth is that Jesus is being sold out and merchandised, and the apostolic ministry is being turned into a marketplace for prostitution and casual harlotry. We have replaced authentic apostolic fathering with apostolic networking, and it is deeply grieving the heart of God. The new apostolic generation will contend for intimate love and relationship with fathers as demonstrated by Paul the Apostle. They will not settle for shallow marketing techniques and illicit spiritual favors.

The Shepherding Movement Reborn

I received another prophetic dream in that same season of intense prayer and fasting, concerning apostolic ministry in the earth, where the Spirit of God specifically showed me that over the next twenty years we are going to see the "Shepherding Movement" of the 1970's REBORN, through false and soulish apostolic leaders in America, who will specifically prey upon this fatherless generation of young people.

There is a deceiving apostolic wineskin currently operating in the body of Christ that believes that individuals who do not submit to their authority are wounded, rebellious, and prideful. This soulish apostolic company thrives on titles, showmanship, control, intimidation, fear and releasing "new revelation" that must be swallowed by their followers.

Their over-emphases will be the same as those in the 1970's, namely: authority, submission, and accountability, all of which are biblical truths that will be blown out of proportion and hammered upon the next generation.

In the midst of this coming apostolic deception, we must not lose sight of true apostolic fathers who, through love and care, will properly impart both their own lives and revelation of Jesus Christ, and raise up and release genuine sons and daughters. Many of the true apostolic fathers in the coming days will be relatively unknown to many, and will give birth to true sons like Timothy, who will be the true five-fold ministry leaders that this generation so desperately needs!

We must have true voices in the body of Christ who will not compromise their DNA for the sake of connectivity and platforms. Forging friendships with one another with the hidden motivation of seeking greater visibility and notoriety is idolatry. There are many unholy alliances forming among church leaders. The religious apostolic games need to stop. Let's get back to private devotion with Jesus and move beyond the public prostitution of gifting and notoriety.

The new apostolic generation will discover their voice in the wilderness, not from being connected to another network. A soulish search for validation and significance has driven too many out of the wilderness and into the arms of soulish and false apostles, who are looking to prey upon the next generation. In the years ahead, we are going to witness the shaking and dismantling of apostolic networking like never before. Motives, attitudes, and the flesh are going to be exposed, and what has been built upon the altar of performance and greed will be burned in the fire. From up out of the ashes and rubble will come a generation of sons and daughters, who will find their identity, purpose, and destiny from their Father in heaven. They will be a mighty force in the kingdom of God and resolve to know nothing but Jesus Christ and Him crucified.

Apostolic Elitism

The body of Christ is a one-bodied, many-membered, and different-functioning organism that is full of the life and diversity of God. There are different callings and giftings upon the sons and daughters, each according to the grace given by God Himself. Paul specifically chooses to address those members who are WEAKER among us, as he says they are "necessary" and "when they suffer, we all suffer" (1 Cor 12:22;26). It is clear in the Scriptures that we are never given permission as church leaders to throw away those saints among us who are sick, hurting, broken, or simply do not run at the same pace as we do. It only takes a simple perusal of the gospels to understand that Jesus came not for the well, but those in need. Besides, He walked the earth and chose 12 poor and uneducated fisherman to fulfill His will, not 12 fiery zealots who had everything together from the start.

There is a rising trend of apostles, and apostolic teams, who are not known as Paul was for being patient with the weak, but militant, harsh, and operate in a "takeover" type mentality. They constantly tell people to find the group of people who understands them the most, and to stay away from certain people. Here are five signs of apostolic elitism for the new apostolic generation to beware of :

1. The apostle, or apostolic team, is constantly surrounded by people that are not hurting, broken, and wounded. Apostolic elitism does not have time for people that just

can't seem to get healed or delivered in a revival service.

Apostolic elitism hides in green rooms and isolates itself

away from those who could ask questions and bring a

different perspective. Apostolic elitism does not have

patience for the hurting, and bashes counseling;

concluding people just need quick-fix deliverance.

2. The apostle or apostolic team is continually preaching

messages in a "us versus them" context. They thrive on

convincing you that most everyone is out to get you, and

there is some type of demonic spirit trying to oppress you

24/7. Those who sit under apostolic elitism will find

themselves constantly paranoid and fearful of what

spiritual attack is coming next.

3. The apostle, or apostolic team, is bent on warning you

of every other leader or stream in the body of Christ. Their

offense becomes your offense. Who they don't like, you

better not like. Apostolic elitism demands your allegiance

and loyalty, and will consider you a traitor if you get advice and input from anyone else but them. Apostolic elitism demands a monthly fee and will disassociate with you if you do not pay your dues.

4. The apostle, or apostolic team, is always encouraging you to cut off relationships in your life that aren't benefitting you. They don't have time for hurting and broken people, so you shouldn't either. Opportunities to love difficult people are called "toxic relationships". Apostolic elitism gives you spiritual language that grants you permission to discontinue friendships and relationships with people.

5. The apostle, and apostolic team, are islands of revelation unto themselves. Apostolic elitism has a spiritual revelation for every concern brought to it. When it is questioned, it comes up with a new revelation for why it was just asked a question. Apostolic elitism is not well

connected to the body of Christ, because it believes it owns the street corner on revival and the kingdom of God, and can't be told what to do. Beware of this kind of arrogance and pride.

The Days Ahead

The need for true apostolic fathers has never been greater in the body of Christ. Fathering is at the heart of all genuine apostolic ministry. We are going to see true apostles rise with the healing balm of Gilead, who through deep love and relationship, will speak into the lives of the generations to come. Christopher Johnson writes and says, "Apostolic ministry and grace is not for tearing people down, nor for controlling people, not for telling people what to do, not for fulfilling one's own secret ambitions, not for having preeminence over others, and not for making one's self indispensable. It is for the building up of the lives and hearts of others." (The Fullness of Ministry, Fishnet Publications 2015 page 160)

Apostolic fathers will emerge that will be accessible, humble, and full of the love of God the Father for His children. The new apostolic generation is destined to be fathered by no-named apostolic fathers who can't give them a platform or open up a national door for them, but they can impart love and life at a deeper level than most have ever known. The apostolic merry-go-round has provided a false sense of identity and connection for too many people with impure motives. As apostolic fathering takes place, we must beware of any form of elitism or a rebirth of the shepherding movement. The devil never counterfeits trash and he knows how powerful apostolic fathering can be in a generation. Let the true apostolic fathers rise in this hour, and let the new apostolic generation be warned of deceptive and soulish practices among those who are claiming to be apostles, but are not.

Beware of the Religious Spirit

Has the religious spirit disguised itself and is now trying to move from pastors and their denominations to apostles and their networks? I meet hundreds of saints every year who are coming out of large denominational churches hurting, broken, and disillusioned. Upon personally interviewing hundreds of them, they primarily cite their reasons for leaving as two main issues: 1. An Overemphasis on Tithes/Offerings. 2. Pastor was non-relational and controlling.

Where have all these people now transferred to? Sure some of them have just stopped going to church all together, but the strange and interesting trend I have been observing over the last ten years is this: People that are leaving larger denominational churches by the droves, are now joining all these "networks", and are seeking to place themselves under an "apostle".

In many cases, we have now replaced being connected to a "local church" to now being connected to a "network". And we have now replaced being submitted to a "pastor" to now being submitted to an "apostle." Instead of giving our money to the local church, we now give our money to a network. And instead of serving under a pastor, we now serve under an apostle. Does anyone else see the problem or trend within this epidemic?

I want to sound the alarm and prophetically declare that many saints are just transferring from one form of religion to the next; from a religious local church to a religious apostolic network, and from a controlling pastor to a controlling apostle. Neither one of these realities is what God has prepared for the new apostolic generation! True apostolic fathering that is relational, free of charge, empowering, and centered on Christ will be resurrected in

this generation and is clearly seen in the New Testament.

-7-
Apostolic Christianity

As I continue to search the Scriptures and seek God in prayer, I'm now more convinced than ever that apostolic Christianity is the only wineskin that can host the new wine God is pouring out in this generation. Denominational structures, and the institutional nature of them, will continue to hinder, and in most cases, altogether quench the spirit of revival and awakening that is coming upon the body of Christ.

We are going to see the planting of churches by true apostolic fathers who will lay Jesus Christ as the foundation, cornerstone, and head of His Church. These apostles will establish a plurality of elders who are going to operate in the five-fold ministry together and train, equip, and release the saints like never before. The new apostolic generation is going to cry out to church leaders

and apostles who operate in a Saul spirit and declare, God

says "Let My People Go". This confrontation and cry will

be heard throughout the ages. One-man ministries are

going to crumble all over the earth because they cannot

contain the new wine God is pouring out. As eldership

teams govern local churches together, the five-fold

ministry will begin to function like never before. Rather

than receiving from only one man every week, the saints of

God will become apostolic, prophetic, evangelistic,

pastoral, and a teaching people as they receive from all

five ministries in their midst. "Only then can the body of

Christ begin to attain to the unity of the faith, and of the

knowledge of the Son of God, to a mature man, to the

measure of the stature which belongs to the fullness of

Christ." (Eph 4:13)

In the days and years ahead, I believe a generation

of Martin Luther's (reformers) are going to revolt against denominations and religious structures, and form a wineskin of apostolic Christianity that will host the new wine being poured out. To the surprise of many, numerous church leaders that carry this type of "Martin Luther" reformation anointing are currently referred to as "pastors and teachers " within their denominations and religious structures, because there is no revelation or embrace of apostles, prophets, or apostolic Christianity. Many of these church leaders know that God has called them as an apostle or prophet and that they should be operating in a team of elders. I believe God is now releasing them to teach apostolic Christianity straight out of the Gospels and the book of Acts (and not from a church growth textbook), but they are unsure concerning what will happen if they make the shift. Some of them are "senior pastors" with a board and have finally recognized that its not even biblical.

God is going to strengthen these church leaders with the power of His might, and confirm His word, as they shift and begin to obey Him.

Remember, in 1517 Martin Luther nailed the paper containing his 95 theses to the church doors in Wittenberg and started the Protestant Reformation. All he sought was a debate, but little did he know he was starting a fire that would burn through the ages! The Father's decree in heaven of "Let My People Go" is more than a debate, we are talking about a fire that could potentially burn through denominations and religious thinking and structures forever.

The new apostolic generation emerging will be a generation of pioneers and reformers that will pay a hefty price for the convictions that they hold so dearly. Their desire for restoring biblical foundations that have been lost throughout the centuries will stir up the religious spirit like never before. They will cry out for Jesus Christ to be exalted and receive pre-eminence in all things. The new apostolic generation will weep and groan at the worship of men and their ministries. The fire they carry will expose the dryness of the Saul's around them.

Five-fold ministry leaders who carry a Davidic heart of humility and teamwork will train and equip the body of Christ like never before. While all five ministries of apostles, prophets, teachers, shepherds, and evangelists are needed in this hour, be on the lookout for a special connection specifically between apostles, prophets, and intercessors as they seek to restore and recover what has been lost.

Apostles, Prophets, and Intercessors

The kingdom of God is powerfully established and advanced when apostles, prophets, and intercessors each work together in the specific function/assignment that God has given them. When unified, and operating with clarity, these three groups tear down demonic strongholds and plant and establish the kingdom of God in the earth. Let's look closely at how they partner together.

The Prophets

The prophets receive and release the "words and heart of God" through dreams, visions, and other means to apostles and intercessors. Prophets save and spare apostles and intercessors from UNNECESSARY LABOR AND WARFARE! Rather than intercessors trying to dig for revelation and insight, prophets give it to them with little to no time wasted. This allows intercessors to engage in "informed prayer" or "prophetic intercession". Prophets also release the word of the Lord to apostles, which oftentimes simply confirms what the apostles are receiving in prayer and study of God's Word. Many apostles are waiting to put things into motion until they get a witness from a prophetic voice. They view it as permission and confirmation to move forward.

The Apostles

The apostles are called to MOBILIZE and put into MOTION the word and heart of God. This is why it is so important that apostles are working in close relationship with the prophets. The prophet will see "in part", and the apostle will come and bring a "fullness" perspective to what the prophet has seen. Prophets carry the gift of vision, but oftentimes lack the administrative gifting that apostles carry. Apostles call forth the intercessors and have them begin to mobilize the word of the Lord through strategic prayer assignments and covering of leaders and their families. True prophets are a blessing to apostles and help protect them from becoming rigid, legalistic, controlling, and authoritarian. Prophets are called to keep apostles from functioning from the position of the "letter that kills", and move them to the place of "the Spirit that gives life." Prophets must work closely together with apostles so that blind spots can be revealed.

The Intercessors

When intercessors are not connected to true apostles and prophets, they will grow tired, weary, and disillusioned. Many of them who are simply connected to shepherds (pastors) will at times become convinced that they are going crazy. Most intercessors are familiar with giving the word of the Lord to "their pastor", but have never really been led by apostles and prophets who give them the word of the Lord. Intercessors help advance the plans and purposes of God by standing in the gap and declaring the word of the Lord. They also help to mobilize and put into motion the promises of God by stirring up communities of believers to wake up and get involved.

I believe that the misunderstanding of how apostles, prophets, and intercessors are supposed to be working together has seriously hindered the establishing and advancing of the kingdom of God. At its core, PRIDE is the greatest enemy of these three groups working together, because at times, they are all convinced that they are carrying the greatest revelation and strategy that no one else has. May God release a spirit of humility and purity that is necessary for the advancing of the kingdom of God.

The Teachers are Arising

One of the greatest needs of the hour is for five-fold ministry "Teachers" to arise, full of the Holy Ghost and fire. I'm talking about Teachers who are sound in doctrine, know the Bible frontwards and backwards, and feed the body of Christ meat, not croutons. I'm praying for Teachers who will root and ground this generation in the Word of God, verse upon verse, precept upon precept, full of unction because they actually have a prayer life. We must have anointed Bible Teachers in this generation who when they speak, the people's heads turn and they say, "We have never heard anyone teach with this kind of authority." (Mark 1:21-28).

I want to encourage all the five-fold ministry "Teachers" in the body of Christ to function with unction! We don't need any more people chasing and posing like wannabee "Apostles" and "Prophets" because they think it's cool and popular. Be who God called you to be and don't be ashamed of it one bit!

It's totally okay that people don't fall down in the altars when you pray for them, that you don't give out prophecies like candy, or you don't see crazy miracles all the time. Trust me, there is a growing number of Charismatics tired of all fire tunnels, prophecy lines, and pushing people down in the altars. They just want someone to actually exegete passages of Scripture without taking them out of context, or adding some weird experience to it and calling it "revelation".

Just teach and handle the Word of God with integrity and clarity. You are a tremendous blessing and greatly needed in this generation who is chasing after the wind and their feelings. I'm with you, praying for you, and I believe all of heaven has its eyes open you in this hour. Teach!

A Prophetic Blessing

As an elder and apostolic father in the body of Christ, I would like to give my prophetic blessing to the new apostolic generation that is emerging. I would have never been able to write this book without God taking me to heaven and revealing His blueprint in the Scriptures in the years that followed. I recognize that many church leaders just do not understand the fire and passion rising in young people all over the earth. There are signs and deep stirrings that the greatest outpouring of the Holy Spirit that we have ever seen is quickly upon us. The new wine is coming, but will it fall into an old wineskin of a one-man ministry building their own kingdom and dreams? The new apostolic generation is hungry to know and experience Jesus like never before. They will walk in pure and simple hearted devotion to their Lord and Savior. They are longing for authentic apostolic fathering, and the restoration of the five-fold ministry in the earth. They are ready to be trained, equipped, and sent!

New apostolic generation, I bless you and I thank

God for you! I bless your courage and desire to build the house of God not according to the traditions of men, but according to the pattern laid out in the Scriptures. I bless you as church leaders operating in a Saul spirit will curse you, accuse you, and speak all kinds of evil against you. I bless your hunger to be trained, equipped, and sent, rather than sit on a pew the rest of your life. I bless you to connect with the true apostolic fathers, most of them who are not well-known and cannot offer you platforms and popularity. I bless you to walk in healing and honor towards those who don't understand you or the call on your life. I bless you with special grace to walk in humility and stay clear of pride that will cause God to resist you. As you build the house of God and create the wineskin that will hold the new wine being poured out in the earth, I bless you to decrease so that the hunger and pre-eminence of Jesus Christ might increase.

New apostolic generation, I am praying for you and I believe in you. My greatest heart's desire is that, just as the ninety-five theses were nailed at Wittenberg in 1517 that started the Protestant Reformation, so this book in some small way might be nailed to the doors of our hearts and the global Church, and start an Apostolic Reformation the likes we have never seen before. May the words in these pages bring life, encouragement, hope, correction, fresh fire, and language to what is burning inside of your hearts. The best is yet to come. You were born for such a time as this!

With all my love and affection in Christ Jesus,

Jeremiah Johnson

Maranatha School of Ministry

More than writing a book, I have received a mandate from the Father in heaven to open up and oversee a 3 year full time school of ministry in Lakeland, FL starting in August of 2018. With a wonderful facility dedicated just for Maranatha School of Ministry, I and several other faculty members will begin training and equipping students from all over the United States and world on a full time basis. The facility is currently connected to Heart of the Father Ministry and will allow students to be on campus throughout the year. The 3 year school of ministry will cover subjects such as:

-Jesus Christ as the Foundation and Head of His Church

-The Five Fold Ministry

-Plurality of Eldership

-The Centrality of God's Word

-Church Planting

-The Prophetic Anointing

-Gifts of the Holy Spirit

-Intimacy with God

-Prayer and Intercession

Maranatha School of Ministry will hold weekly student chapels, outreaches, hours in the prayer room, ministry trips, and classroom intensives and lectures.

For more information and to submit your application into the school, please call (863) 940 2867.

About the Author

Jeremiah Johnson received his God given name through a prophetic dream his mother had while he was in her womb. God said that he would be a prophetic messenger and dreamer to the nations, but great complications would mark his birth. Months later, Jeremiah was delivered dead in the delivery room with the umbilical cord wrapped around his neck. However, God intervened and the medical team was able to save both Jeremiah and his mother's life.

Jeremiah was raised in a Charismatic environment where his father pastored a church outside of Indianapolis, IN for nearly 15 years. From the time he was 7 years old, Jeremiah began receiving regular prophetic encounters from dreams and visions at night, to sharing the word of the Lord as he matured in age. God pouring out His Spirit through miracles, prophecy, signs and wonders, and the five fold ministry were all part of the foundation and heritage that Jeremiah was privileged to be raised in as a child and youth.

Jeremiah graduated from Southeastern University in Lakeland, FL where he earned his bachelors degree in Church Ministries. He entered full time ministry at the age of 20 and has had the privilege of traveling and preaching the Gospel of Jesus Christ and prophesying in more than 20 foreign countries and 35 states.

In 2010, Jeremiah planted Heart of the Father Ministry in Lakeland, FL and currently serves on the Eldership Team full time. This community of believers has grown into a gathering of more than 400 saints hungry for revival, prayer, and a mighty harvest of souls. Along with being one of the Elders at this growing church plant, Jeremiah also travels and ministers to leaders and churches all over the United States and abroad. He carries a prophetic message of encountering Jesus Christ and living a consecrated life unto God in more than 35 churches and conferences a year under his traveling ministry, "Jeremiah Johnson Ministries". To follow Jeremiah, go to: jeremiahjohnson.tv

In 2018, Jeremiah will begin overseeing "Maranatha School of Ministry" on a full time basis. Jeremiah is married to his beautiful wife Morgan and they have three children: Bella Grace, Israel David, and Lydia Joy.

Jeremiah's Other Published Books

-Chronicles of the Unknown Dreamer 2013

-I See A New Prophetic Generation

-The Micaiah Company: A Prophetic

Reformation

To purchase your copies today, please visit:

jeremiahjohnson.tv

Recommended Reads

-The Fullness of Ministry

by Christopher Johnson

-The Church in the New Testament

by Kevin Conner

Made in the USA
Columbia, SC
27 June 2020

12180721R00100